I0418240

Going Viral
Encouraging Words for Discouraging Times

———

Library of Congress Control Number: 2022914671

ISBN: 979-8-9867212-0-0

Edited by M. H. Watkins
Book and Cover Design by Daren Hastings

Published by Wonder Ministries of Wayzata, MN.

An early form of this book was serialized and published on several Facebook group pages moderated by the author between March 22, 2020 and January 21, 2021.

Printed in the USA.

ACKNOWLEDGMENTS

I tried to write this book completely on my own, without any help, but I couldn't do it. A book only becomes a finished product through the collaboration of many talented individuals. All of them deserve thanks.

Here are the people I remember. I'm sure I'll forget someone, and for that I apologize.

I thank my wife Caren and my father Gene — you gave me time to write during a busy and stressful time and I took it, even though it was time I could have spent with you. I love you both more than I can say.

I thank my editor, M. H. Watkins, and designer Daren Hastings — they were among the friends who saw the original Facebook posts. Later they agreed to help me convert those posts into a form that was ready for publication. Your help, input and critical insight made this a much better book. You make a great team and I cannot thank you guys enough!

I thank Ken Churchill, Terry Kerns, Tim Anderson, Pat Misener, Doug Roper, Joel Johnson, Helmar Heckel, Daniel Rakotojoelinandrasana, Gregg Donnelly and Dominic Broda — most of my pastors over my adult life (I'm sure I forgot someone) — for your solid teaching and strong examples of the Christian life.

I thank my communication professors at Crown College in 2007 & 2008, for rekindling my love of writing and putting a bit of polish on my self-taught skills.

I thank my professors at St. Paul Bible College in the mid 1970s, especially the late Dr. Stanton W. Richardson, for not simply teaching me how to study the Bible, but also showing me how a person lives out their Christian faith.

Most of all, I need to thank my Lord and Savior Jesus Christ, for making this book and all things possible.

As Johann Sebastian Bach inscribed all his manuscripts, soli Deo gloria!

"There is nothing to fear but fear itself."   — Franklin D. Roosevelt, from his 1933 inaugural address.

Fear is everywhere. Everyone is afraid of something. Our world is frightening, too. It's scary economically, politically, socially, you-name-it scary. And it doesn't look like things will get much better any time soon. We are living in a pandemic of fear.

Fear is a deeply personal thing. Everyone has different fears. Things that scare me to death may not bother you at all. It's a wonder we can sleep at night.

Fear is a four letter word. That's right, it often is nasty and evil, not to mention a tool of the devil. People often are afraid something new or unexpected. Every single time, according to the Bible, the first words angels say to people are "Don't be afraid." There are times to be afraid, there are also times to be bold and courageous. We know God doesn't want us live in fear, but how do we do that? I wrote this book to answer that question.

Is there a vaccine or antidote for fear? Yes, there is, and it's called love. One of the best ways to show love is encouragement.

Like you, I probably spend more time on Facebook than I should and that was true during the COVID-19 pandemic, too. I saw a lot of fear around me at the time, and in people I know, too, people I thought were stronger than they seemed. This book started as a series of posts between March 22, 2020 and January 21, 2021, on several Facebook group pages that I moderate. Those original posts were meant to encourage my friends. When I realized I knew other people who might benefit from this encouragement, I sent it to them in an email. One Facebook friend had asked permission to reprint my posts in his Facebook feed. The popularity of the public Facebook group skyrocketed. Apparently these "encouraging words," as I called them, were now reaching WAY outside my circle of friends. At some point someone asked if they would be collected into a book. You're holding the answer to that question.

My editor and I did our best to minimize it, but you'll see the terms COVID-19 and coronavirus more than a few times in these pages. When you see those terms, treat them as placeholders for (or symbols of) something that frightens you. People may not be as afraid of COVID-19 now as they were in 2020, but there are still many things to be afraid of.

I dedicate this book to anyone who is struggling to overcome their fears. You need all the encouragement you can get, and I think you can find it in this book.

TABLE OF CONTENTS

We all watch the news. Yesterday's news (March 21) was typical; it was all about the coronavirus (and a few minutes about the late Kenny Rogers). It seems that COVID-19 is all the media wants to talk about. We all have been scared. Maybe you're gone past scared and are numb with fear. Everyone needs encouragement these days. The good news is, you don't have to be a pastor to encourage someone. So I'm going to give it my best shot.

I'm reminded of a verse that was quite popular some time ago, II Chronicles 7:14. "If My people who are called by My name will humble themselves, and pray and seek My face, and turn from their wicked ways, then I will hear from heaven, and will forgive their sin and heal their land." (NKJV) Our land definitely needs healing, so let's break this down.

Obviously God is talking, but to who? He's speaking to His people, those who are called by His name. At the time that was the nation of Israel. The way I understand it, today these people are those who say they believe that God means what He says in the Bible.

What does God want these people to do?

1) Humble themselves. "God opposes the proud but shows favor to the humble." (James 4:6) In short, we need to get our egos under control and remember that only God is God.

2) Pray, which is simply talking to God. If you're anything like me, you probably need to unload what's on your heart or mind to someone, so why not talk to God? I can guarantee He will listen.

3) Seek God's face. Remember playing hide-n-seek as a kid? Seek means more than taking a casual look. Seek means search; there is time and effort involved. People have written sermons and books about seeking God's face, and we should read some of them.

4) Turn from their wicked ways. Maybe you're thinking, "I'm not wicked." If so, my question to you is, "By whose standards?" God has his own standards. He defined them in the book of Exodus, starting in chapter 20. Jesus Christ further explained them in the Gospel of Matthew, chapters 5, 6 and 7. Jesus' message has always been "Repent, for the kingdom of heaven is near." (Matthew 4:17) Acts 20:21 defines repentance as turning

from sin and turning to God. So we need to turn from sin and our wicked ways, and turn to God.

Once these things happen, what does God say he will do?

1) Hear from heaven. What? The Almighty God of the universe will hear us? That's what He said. That in itself is a powerful concept.

2) Forgive their sin. That's great news! I need my sins forgiven, how about you? God's forgiveness is the subject of many other books and sermons; check some out.

3) Heal their land.

Many times we want the healing, but don't want to turn from our wicked ways. That's not going to work, because it doesn't follow God's formula. We have to do it His way or it won't work at all.

Here's my closing thought. This coronavirus situation will last as long as God lets it last. If we truly believe God is in control, then God has power and authority over the coronavirus. So let's beg God to mutate this virus into a harmless variant soon, before it does serious damage to the national and global economy. If we approach Him the way He tells us to, He will listen and heal our land. I am not saying we should ignore health professionals; I'm saying we should put more faith in what God tells us than in what the health professionals say.

Today I heard my pastor preach from II Timothy 1:7, which says, "For God has not given us a spirit of fear, but of power and of love and of a sound mind." So get out from under your beds and get on your knees with me. God WILL beat this virus, if we ask Him to in the right way.

A quick encouraging word tonight, Psalm 121 —

> I lift up my eyes to the mountains— where does my help come from? My help comes from the Lord, the Maker of heaven and earth. He will not let your foot slip— he who watches over you will not slumber; indeed, he who watches over Israel will neither slumber nor sleep. The Lord watches over you— the Lord is your shade at your right hand; the sun will not harm you by day, nor the moon by night. The Lord will keep you from all harm— he will watch over your life; the Lord will watch over your coming and going both now and forevermore.

The "word" I wanted to post is taking longer than I thought it would and will come out Sunday.

WORD 3   He's Coming Back!   3-29-2020

We all know someone who seems to be singing the song Buck Owens and Roy Clark wrote for the old TV show Hee-Haw, "Gloom, despair, and agony on me." (It's on YouTube.) Maybe you're one of those people. I'm writing these pieces to encourage people, and I've decided to tell you the most encouraging thing I know. So get ready, this is going to be good...

Jesus Christ is coming back!

It's true, you know. He promised to come back. And that in itself is encouraging. When the Apostle Paul described Christ's return to the Thessalonian church, he closed it by saying, "Therefore, encourage each another with these words." (I Thess 4:18)

The word "therefore" means this is Paul's conclusion, but to what? Let's back up and start from verse 16 —

> "For the Lord himself will come down from heaven, with a loud command, with the voice of the archangel and with the trumpet call of God, and the dead in Christ will rise first. After that, we who are still alive and are left will be caught up together with them in the clouds to meet the Lord in the air. And so we will be with the Lord forever. Therefore encourage one another with these words."

So what's encouraging here? I see several things. First, Jesus is coming back for us, whether we're alive or not. Second, those who are alive will be reunited with those who died in Christ, friends and family who went ahead. Third, we will meet Jesus face to face! And finally, all believers, including us, will be with the Lord forever. Isn't that great news? A pastor might ask, "Can I get an amen?"

Yes, Jesus is coming back. He said so Himself several times. The disciples eventually asked Jesus about His return in Matthew 24. What did they ask — "How can this be?" Or maybe "Are you serious?" No, they asked, "What will be the sign of your coming?" (Matt 24:3) They got it! Even before He died, his disciples honestly believed Jesus would return.

The answer Jesus gave in Matthew 24 is both specific and vague. He describes what life will be like for His followers when He returns, but stops short of giving enough detail to determine exactly when He will return.

This is probably because He didn't know, either. In Matthew 24:36 Jesus said, "no one knows, not even the angels of heaven, nor the Son, but the Father only."

Jesus is coming back!

Jesus talked about it, why don't we? We don't have to get tangled up in timelines. (That sounds like something out of a science fiction movie.) Jesus never set up a timeline; people did that and maybe it was a mistake. It makes us focus on the wait instead of what we should do while we're waiting. And isn't the important thing that Jesus promised to come back?

Remember the account of Jesus' last moment on earth in Acts 1? The disciples had asked the 'when' question again.

> "He said to them, 'It is not for you to know the times or dates the Father has set by his own authority. But you will receive power when the Holy Spirit comes on you; and you will be my witnesses in Jerusalem, and in all Judea and Samaria, and to the ends of the earth.' After he said this, he was taken up before their very eyes, and a cloud hid him from their sight. They were looking intently up into the sky as he was going, when suddenly two men dressed in white stood beside them. 'Men of Galilee,' they said, 'why do you stand here looking into the sky? This same Jesus, who has been taken from you into heaven, will come back in the same way you have seen him go into heaven.'"

Jesus is coming back!

When was the last time you read Matthew 24 & 25? Please read it again. It says a lot more good things than what I'll say in this quick summary. The disciples asked Him, "Tell us when this will happen, and what will be the sign of your coming and of the end of the age?" Jesus begins with a description of the conditions his followers will face at that time. He then warns His people to be ready and follows with a parable that reinforces His warning, the parable of the 10 virgins. Next is the parable of the talents, which tells the disciples and us to keep doing what pleases God and furthers His kingdom. Jesus wraps up His teaching with a parable about sheep and goats, which tells us what will happen to those who obey what He's just said and those who don't. Naturally we want to know when it will happen, but to Jesus it is more important that we are both ready and working for His return.

Jesus is coming back!

Remember stories or movies about the frontier days of the USA? Often there is a young couple, either engaged or newly married, who become separated. The man says something like, "I'll go build us a house and set everything up. I'll come back for you as soon as I can." Does that sound familiar? It's exactly what Jesus says to His disciples in John 14:2 & 3 — "My Father's house has many rooms; if that were not so, would I have told you that I am going there to prepare a place for you? And if I go and prepare a place for you, I will come back and take you to be with me that you also may be where I am."

Jesus really is coming back!

I was saved during the Jesus Movement of the late 1960s and early 1970s. Back then we heard and sang songs that reminded us Jesus is coming back. There were a number of them, good songs that stuck in your head. We would not let ourselves forget that Jesus was coming back. These days, though, I wonder if we have forgotten. We have certainly lost that feeling that Jesus could come back at any moment. When did you last hear a song or a sermon about the return of Jesus? If we don't hear about it or talk about it, how can we be encouraged by it? How can we remember it, much less be prepared for it?

Jesus is coming back!

This is what makes Christianity different from any other religion on Earth. Buddha never said anything about coming back and neither did Mohammed, Confucius or anyone else. It is one of the central points of our faith. And Jesus wants us to believe it. He wants us to remember it. He wants us to talk about it. He wants us to be ready for it and to be doing what He wants us to do until He comes.

Yes, things look bad. Jesus said they would in the early verses of Matthew 24. It's one of the signs of what we call the end times. Jesus might come back before this crisis is over. Then again, He might not. It doesn't change the fact that Jesus IS coming back. So encourage each other with these words.

Revelation 22:20 says, "He who testifies to these things says, 'Yes, I am coming soon.' Amen. Come, Lord Jesus."

Jesus is coming back! Make some noise — Hallelujah! Praise God!

Want some more encouragement? I promise this one will be shorter than the last one.

You have an incredible superpower. You have access to the infinite power of the Almighty God of the universe. If that's not a superpower, I don't know what is, and I'm a comic book fan.

You want proof? I've got it. John 15:7 & 8 — "If you remain in me and my words remain in you, ask whatever you wish, and it will be done for you. This is to my Father's glory, that you bear much fruit, showing yourselves to be my disciples."

Our power is conditional. That means we need to do something in order to get our power. We need to remain in Christ and we need His words to remain in us. We also need to bear fruit and show ourselves to be His disciples. Jesus is saying we need to be about the glory of God. Only then can we ask whatever we wish, and it will be done for us.

Also, there's Matthew 21:21-22 — "Jesus replied, 'Truly I tell you, if you have faith and do not doubt, not only can you do what was done to the fig tree, but also you can say to this mountain, 'Go, throw yourself into the sea,' and it will be done. If you believe, you will receive whatever you ask for in prayer.'"

These verses say we need to believe, to have faith and no doubt. The obvious question is, believe in what? More accurately, believe in whom? We need to believe Jesus Christ is not simply the Son of God, He is God in flesh —

> "My goal is that they may be encouraged in heart and united in love, so that they may have the full riches of complete understanding, in order that they may know the mystery of God, namely, Christ, in whom are hidden all the treasures of wisdom and knowledge... For in Christ all the fullness of the Deity lives in bodily form."   (Colossians 2:2-3, 9)

Now check out Matthew 18:19-20 — "Again, truly I tell you that if two of you on earth agree about anything they ask for, it will be done for them by my Father in heaven. For where two or three gather in my name, there am I with them." That means we superheroes need to team up! This saying applies to prayer, too — there is strength in numbers.

Now look at Luke 11:9-10, where Jesus said, "So I say to you: Ask and it will be given to you; seek and you will find; knock and the door will be opened to you. For everyone who asks receives; the one who seeks finds; and to the one who knocks, the door will be opened."

We looked at 2 Chronicles 7:14 earlier. It talks about how to make prayer work: "If my people, who are called by my name, will humble themselves and pray and seek my face and turn from their wicked ways, then I will hear from heaven, and I will forgive their sin and will heal their land." This time my point is that humbling ourselves, praying, seeking God's face and turning from our wicked ways will unleash God's power.

I'll say it again — that sure sounds like a superpower to me! And I know just how we can use it, too. Let's ask God to change this coronavirus into something harmless, and the sooner, the better.

"Home, home on the range, where the deer and the antelope play. Where seldom is heard a discouraging word..."

It seems that all we hear on the news about this coronavirus pandemic is discouraging words. There aren't enough medical supplies, the stores are out of hand sanitizer or bread or toilet paper or something, the death count is up and things are going to get worse. I've had enough of discouraging words, how about you? The encouraging word for today is hope.

As Christians, what is our hope? On what do we base our hope? People have written books on that! I'll try to give a short but meaningful answer.

Our hope is based on God, His power and love and promises. That's where it all starts. We need a personal experience with the power of God. We need to know not only that God has the power to keep His promises, but also that He DOES keep His promises. Seeing the Holy Spirit at work in the Bible, in history, in people around us and in our lives shows us God's power and gives us hope. Our hope comes from a confident assurance that God will do what He has promised.

I could give you a list of verses and expound on them, but I won't. Sometimes it's easier to understand something by looking at what it is not. Can you remember a time when you were without hope or had lost hope? I can. It will be a long time before I forget...

Back in May 2008 I lost my dream job. It was a series of contract positions, so I knew it could end, but because the company had renewed my contract twice I hoped they would hire me. That didn't happen. You probably remember 2008. The economy went WAY down the tubes. President Obama extended unemployment benefits, meaning they lasted longer than they normally would have, which to me was a good thing, because nobody seemed to want my skills. I managed to pick up some seasonal work over the next couple years. My wife and I were barely keeping our heads above water, as the saying goes.

In the summer of 2011, after three years of looking, I gave up on finding another full time job. I put just enough effort into my so-called job search to keep getting unemployment checks, but really didn't expect anything to happen. When I prayed for work, my heart wasn't in it. I kept myself somewhat busy but was literally wasting time by not doing anything of value or productive. I was even praying God would take me to be with Him in Heaven.

When November 2011 arrived, my wife and I were at the end of our financial rope. In an effort to keep the house I tried to refinance it. I found out you need to have a job before you can refinance your house. That didn't help my already dark mood. I was over 50 and thinking age discrimination was taking me out of consideration for many jobs I was qualified to do, but of course I couldn't prove it. My faith was weak and my hope was long gone. By this time I had been out of work for about 3 ½ years. One day my wife and I sat down (okay, she sat me down) to go over our financial situation. We were getting dangerously close to our last dollar. I had another seasonal job coming up in December, but we couldn't wait that long. We needed help before the month was over.

Do you know what a cold resume is? It's basically a letter of introduction, a resume you send to a company when you have no idea if they need someone like you or not. We knew about a printed circuit board manufacturing company that employed several people I had worked with at another PCB shop in the past. My wife thought I should let them know about me. I didn't want to. I wanted to be done with the PCB industry, because it's barely surviving in this country. We went back and forth about it for a while. I eventually sent them a cold resume a month earlier, so she would quit nagging me about it. At least it felt like nagging at the time...

God had mercy on my wife. That resume went to a couple of their supervisors before the company called me about an opening involving a skill I hadn't used for over 20 years. After I interviewed for that job, they invited me back to interview for another job! They offered me this second job, which completely blew my puny human mind. I gratefully accepted.

My point is that God is faithful and He does keep his promises. When I had hit rock bottom, gave up on myself and wanted to end it all, God had mercy on my wife (and me) and gave me that second job. The challenges and frustrations of the job not only keep me humble, they remind me I don't deserve this job. I've seen the power of God and His love in my life. I didn't deserve it; I am not worthy. He did it anyway. That's what gives me hope in these dark days. God took me through the darkness before; He can do it again.

Call me Barnabas for the next few minutes, even though my name is Carl. Barnabas means "son of encouragement." That's who I want to be, a son of encouragement to you.

When you think of peace, what comes to mind? Sitting in a lounge chair by a calm lake, maybe with a fishing pole in your hand? Maybe you're in the mountains, watching a creek slowly and gently meander down the slope. Maybe it's an hour after sunset and you're seeing hundreds of stars sparkle in a pristine black sky. Maybe it's simply an hour without the kids? At one time or another, all of those options have their appeal.

When Bible talks about the peace of God, it's talking about an inner peace or calmness, not a peace between you and an opponent. Most of Paul's letters begin with the words "Grace and peace to you from God our Father and the Lord Jesus Christ." He also says peace is a fruit of the Spirit (Galatians 5:22). So how do we get this peace? Where does it come from? Let's look at some verses together.

The apostle Peter once said, "Grace and peace be yours in abundance through the knowledge of God and of Jesus our Lord." (2 Peter 1:2) Did you catch that? Both Peter and Paul tell us where peace comes from. Paul said it comes "from God our Father and the Lord Jesus Christ." Peter agrees, but goes a bit further — "through the knowledge of God and of Jesus our Lord." So the more we know about God and Jesus, the more abundant our peace will be.

"Let the peace of Christ rule in your hearts, since as members of one body you were called to peace." Colossians 3:15

That body, the body of Christ, is the church. As members of His body we are not only called to peace, we need to let His peace rule in our hearts. It's hard for people to see that we are part of Jesus' body when we don't let that peace rule in our hearts.

The idea that peace comes from God has been around for a while. Check out these quotes —

"The LORD gives strength to his people; the LORD blesses his people with peace." Psalm 29:11

"I will listen to what God the LORD says; he promises peace to his people, his faithful servants— but let them not turn to folly." Psalm 85:8

"Great peace have those who love your law, and nothing can make them stumble." Psalm 119:165

"You will keep in perfect peace those whose minds are steadfast, because they trust in you." Isaiah 26:3

Sounds great, doesn't it? But you need to notice and understand everything God wants here. We need to love God's law and not turn to folly. And we need a steadfast mind. Steadfast means firm or resolute and it's linked with trust. Our minds are steadfast because we trust God. We need to resolve to keep our minds on God and believe He is in control, no matter what happens. The result is a supernatural peace, the kind that people are looking for, especially in these troubled times.

"Peace I leave with you; my peace I give you. I do not give to you as the world gives. Do not let your hearts be troubled and do not be afraid." (John 14:27)

Did you hear that? Jesus gives us His peace. He offers it to us; He wants us to have it. Troubled hearts and fears can take away your peace, though.

Now look at some of the benefits of God's peace —

"The peace of God, which transcends all understanding, will guard your hearts and your minds in Christ Jesus." Philippians 4:7

"Peacemakers who sow in peace reap a harvest of righteousness." James 3:18

"I have told you these things, so that in me you may have peace. In this world you will have trouble. But take heart! I have overcome the world." John 16:33

"For the kingdom of God is not a matter of eating and drinking, but of righteousness, peace and joy in the Holy Spirit, because anyone who serves Christ in this way is pleasing to God and receives human approval. Let us therefore make every effort to do what leads to peace and to mutual edification." Romans 14:17-19

Jesus offers us His peace and tells us what we need to do to keep it. Yes, that takes work, but the end results are worth it — for us as individuals, for our churches and for the people around us who desperately need the peace we can have. Peace be with you, my friends!

WORD 7   Because He Lives   4-12-2020

Today is Easter Sunday, so happy Easter, everyone! Not even the nefarious coronavirus could cancel Easter. That's good news, but I have even better news for you — Jesus is alive. ALIVE!

Some of you sang about it during your church service this morning. Jesus is alive! Mine didn't have enough of those songs, so I put on more after it was over. Christ my Lord is risen today! Now that's encouraging.

We all know or are related to someone who would say, "Big whoop — so what?" What is so good about Jesus coming back to life? You've come to the right place, my friends. I'm going to tell you.

Let's start with the first thing Jesus said to his disciples after the resurrection. Before He died, Jesus said in John 7:33, "I am with you for only a short time, and then I am going to the one who sent me." After He rose from the dead, however, He said in Matthew 28:17 &20, "All authority in heaven and on earth has been given to me... surely I am with you always, to the very end of the age." Because Jesus is alive, He is always with us. Look at those words again: "I am with you always." That's more than a promise, Jesus is stating a fact. And He can say that because He has "all authority in heaven and on earth."

Because Jesus is alive we can be born again! "Praise be to the God and Father of our Lord Jesus Christ! In his great mercy he has given us new birth into a living hope through the resurrection of Jesus Christ from the dead." (I Peter 1:3) And also in Romans 6:4 — "We were therefore buried with him through baptism into death in order that, just as Christ was raised from the dead through the glory of the Father, we too may live a new life." Of course, we need to act on His word in order to be born again. Jesus told us in John 3:5 & 6, "No one can enter the kingdom of God unless they are born of water and the Spirit. Flesh gives birth to flesh, but the Spirit gives birth to spirit."

Because Jesus is alive His teaching must be true! Look at this excerpt from Romans 1: 1 & 4. "Paul, a servant of Christ Jesus... who through the Spirit of holiness was appointed the Son of God in power by his resurrection from the dead." This tells us who Jesus of Nazareth truly is, the Son of God in power. Of course Jesus was the Son of God before His resurrection. The fact that Jesus is alive validates and empowers everything He told us before He died. Without the resurrection all His teaching is empty words.

Because Jesus is alive we will live again! Check out 2 Corinthians 4:14 — "we know that the one who raised the Lord Jesus from the dead <u>will also raise us</u> with Jesus and present us with you to himself." (Yes, I underlined those words.) God will do it. That's a promise! We don't have to be afraid of dying.

I'm going to let the following verses speak for themselves.

Ephesians 2:4-7: "But because of his great love for us, God, who is rich in mercy, made us alive with Christ even when we were dead in transgressions... And God raised us up with Christ and seated us with him in the heavenly realms in Christ Jesus."

Romans 5:9-10: "Since we have now been justified by his [Jesus] blood, how much more shall we be saved from God's wrath through him! For if, while we were God's enemies, we were reconciled to him through the death of his Son, how much more, having been reconciled, shall we be saved through his life!"

There is more, a lot more. The apostle Paul goes to the heart of the matter in 1 Corinthians 15, which is more than I want to quote here. You have a Bible, please read it slowly and carefully. Paul packed a LOT of good stuff in there, such as...

The last thing Jesus said to His disciples is recorded in Acts 1:9: "You will receive power when the Holy Spirit comes on you; and you will be my witnesses." This tells us three things happen because He lives.

> 1) *The Holy Spirit will come upon you.* Because Jesus Christ is alive, we have the Holy Spirit. He told us, "I will ask the Father, and he will give you another advocate to help you and be with you forever." (John 14:16)

> 2) *You will receive power.* What kind of power? The power to be His witnesses, which could mean a lot of things. That's enough about power for now; my point is we get power in our lives because Jesus Christ is alive.

> 3) *You will be my witnesses.* What does that mean? The word witness comes from legal procedure, where a judge will say to a lawyer, "Call your witnesses." These witnesses tell the judge and jury what he or she saw or knows to be true. That's what Jesus wants; we need to tell others the truth about Him.

Bill & Gloria Gaither summarize it very well in their exquisite song "Because He Lives." Google it, read the lyrics and listen to the song. It's well worth the extra effort.

All because Jesus is alive! If that's not encouraging, I don't know what will touch you.

Today's encouraging word is Psalm 34. I like the NIV —

> "I will extol the LORD at all times; his praise will always be on my lips. I will glory in the LORD; let the afflicted hear and rejoice. Glorify the LORD with me; let us exalt his name together.

> "I sought the LORD, and he answered me; he delivered me from all my fears. Those who look to him are radiant; their faces are never covered with shame. This poor man called, and the LORD heard him; he saved him out of all his troubles. The angel of the LORD encamps around those who fear him, and he delivers them.

> "Taste and see that the LORD is good; blessed is the one who takes refuge in him. Fear the LORD, you his holy people, for those who fear him lack nothing. The lions may grow weak and hungry, but those who seek the LORD lack no good thing. Come, my children, listen to me; I will teach you the fear of the LORD. Whoever of you loves life and desires to see many good days, keep your tongue from evil and your lips from telling lies. Turn from evil and do good; seek peace and pursue it.

> "The eyes of the LORD are on the righteous, and his ears are attentive to their cry; but the face of the LORD is against those who do evil, to blot out their name from the earth.

> "The righteous cry out, and the LORD hears them; he delivers them from all their troubles. The LORD is close to the brokenhearted and saves those who are crushed in spirit. The righteous person may have many troubles, but the LORD delivers him from them all; he protects all his bones, not one of them will be broken.

> "Evil will slay the wicked; the foes of the righteous will be condemned. The LORD will rescue his servants; no one who takes refuge in him will be condemned."

In a nutshell, God is powerful and faithful to deliver us, no matter what troubles we are facing. That's good news!

WORD 9   Afraid? Me?   4-19-2020

Remember watching horror movies when you were younger? Or going through a spook house? You managed to endure these tensions and terrors for the next hour or two. You faced the things you feared and escaped unharmed. You always went with at least one friend, though, because having someone with you somehow made it less scary. There's something cathartic about the experience — once it's over.

You've realized by now that my subject for today is fear. I've been told that the Bible says "don't be afraid" or something like it 365 times. Back in school, when the teacher repeated something, that meant it was important and would be on the test. Do you think God is trying to tell us something here?

Let's look at some of these passages and see what we can learn from them.

"Do not be afraid. Stand firm and you will see the deliverance the Lord will bring you today." (Exodus 14:13) Moses said this to his fellow Hebrews when the armies of Pharaoh had them backed up to the Red Sea with no apparent means of escape. You know what happened next, don't you? Sometimes God leads us into situations that turn bad and look inescapable. Do we stay or do we go? When we stand firm where God wants us, He will deliver us.

"Be strong and courageous... the LORD himself goes before you and will be with you; he will never leave you nor forsake you. Do not be afraid; do not be discouraged." (Deuteronomy 31:7-8) This is part of what Moses said to Joshua when Joshua was commissioned as the next leader of Israel. We don't have to be afraid because God goes before us and is with us, and because "He will never leave you nor forsake you," which may sound familiar because it's quoted in Hebrew 13:5.

"Be strong and courageous, and do the work. Do not be afraid or discouraged, for the Lord God, my God, is with you. He will not fail you or forsake you until all the work for the service of the temple of the Lord is finished." (I Chronicles 28:20) King David said this to his son Solomon when he gave him the plans for the temple. Sometimes what God wants us to do looks impossibly huge, but because God is with us, because He will not fail or forsake us, we don't have to be afraid.

"Be strong and courageous. Do not be afraid or discouraged because of the king of Assyria and the vast army with him, for there is a greater power with us than with him. With him is only the arm of flesh, but with us is the Lord our God to help us and to fight our battles." (2 Chronicles 32:7-8) Let me set the scene for you: King Hezekiah had organized the population to rebuild the city of Jerusalem. The king of Assyria decided to conquer them right before the work was finished, so he wouldn't have to invest too much into repairs. The people were worn out from two big projects, the rebuilding and taking care of their families. King Hezekiah reminded them (and us) that there is a greater power with us than with our enemy — "with us is the Lord our God to help us and to fight our battles." The Apostle John echoes this in 1 John 4:4, "You, dear children, are from God and have overcome... because the one who is in you is greater than the one who is in the world."

'When hard pressed, I cried to the Lord; he brought me into a spacious place. The Lord is with me; I will not be afraid. What can mere mortals do to me?' (Psalm 118:5-6) Good question — what could other people do to you? They could take away what you have. They could physically or psychologically torture you (enough said), they could even kill you. The psalmist simply said he was hard pressed. We don't know what his dilemma was, but he said, "Because the Lord is with me, I will not be afraid." Even though other people could destroy your body or mind, they could not affect your spiritual relationship with God. I'll grant you that enduring the process would not be fun, but think of the end results. Jesus said the same thing in Matthew 10:28 "Do not be afraid of those who kill the body but cannot kill the soul. Rather, be afraid of the One who can destroy both soul and body in hell." Or, as the Apostle Paul put it, " I eagerly expect and hope that I will in no way be ashamed, but will have sufficient courage so that now as always Christ will be exalted in my body, whether by life or by death. For to me, to live is Christ and to die is gain." (Philippians 1:20-21)

These verses we read came from impossible situations, where there was no escape. The nation of Israel faced powerful enemies and overwhelming tasks more than once. God's followers have faced physical dangers of many kinds many times. We face the same things today. We need to remember something David said before Goliath moved to attack him: "It is not by sword or spear that the LORD saves; for the battle is the LORD's." (1 Samuel 17:47) This coronavirus is only the latest in the series, and God wants us to collect the whole set, as the saying goes. We need to remember the catchy chorus from Keith Green's song "He'll Take Care of the Rest," which you can find on YouTube, and apply it to our lives.

One of the most popular passages of Scripture is the 23rd Psalm. Many people turn to it when they are looking for comfort. Let's do that tonight and make sure we know what it means, too. I'm going to switch from my usual NIV to the KJV, which is how many of us learned this psalm.

> "The LORD is my shepherd; I shall not want. He maketh me to lie down in green pastures: he leadeth me beside the still waters."

A shepherd provides for his sheep. That's the main point. He guides them to good places where their needs will be met, like green pastures and quiet pools of water. He avoids barren locations without good grass or dangerous places with fast running water.

> "He restoreth my soul: he leadeth me in the paths of righteousness for his name's sake."

Have you ever restored a piece of furniture? It's not fun, but can be rewarding. You start by giving it a good cleaning. Then you evaluate what you see, in order to decide what needs to be done. Some things might need repair before you go any further. Next you strip off the old finish. That may involve a LOT of sanding and/ or stinky and strong chemicals, sometimes both, so you need to protect yourself as well as any fabric on this piece of furniture, unless you also plan to replace the fabric. Chemical strippers don't remove the old finish, either. It doesn't simply fall off; you have to scrape it off. Then you need to seal the wood before you paint or stain it. The sealed surface needs to be smooth, which means more sanding. Now your piece of furniture is ready for a coat or two of wood finish. If you're thinking, "That's a lot of work!" you're right.

God wants to do all that for our worn out souls. For His name's sake, to give honor to His name, He leads his people in the paths of righteousness.

> "Yea, though I walk through the valley of the shadow of death, I will fear no evil: for thou art with me; thy rod and thy staff they comfort me."

The valley of the shadow of death — that sure sounds familiar. The news media is telling us that's where we are right now. The shepherd's rod and staff defend the flock from predators. Seeing Him with them is a comforting sight; that's why we can "fear no evil."

"Thou preparest a table before me in the presence of mine enemies: thou anointest my head with oil; my cup runneth over."

Our enemies are nearby, but we're about to sit down to a feast. We can only do that because that powerful Shepherd is still protecting us. Anointing with oil was done to sanctify or set a person or object apart as holy (Exodus 30:29). A shepherd, however, might use oil to clean the sheep or to treat a wound. And when your cup runs over, you are extremely blessed.

"Surely goodness and mercy shall follow me all the days of my life: and I will dwell in the house of the LORD forever."

We don't see the word "shall" much anymore. It's another form of the verb "should" and can either refer to something in the future or be used instead of "must." Either sense could work here. Notice that "goodness and mercy shall follow" you. They might not be right beside you, but they are not far away. The verse closes in the future — "I will dwell." This verse is a statement of confidence and determination; these things are going to happen.

Psalm 23 is even more comforting when you dig deeper into it, don't you think?

WORD 11   Does Jesus Really Love Me?   4-26-2020

One of the first songs I ever learned goes like this —

"Jesus loves me. This I know, for the Bible tells me so. Little ones to Him belong. They are weak, but He is strong. Yes, Jesus loves me. Yes, Jesus loves me. Yes, Jesus loves me — the Bible tells me so."

Is that true? Does the Bible say God loves us? With all the evil and ugliness in the world around us, does He still love us? Let's find out!

Does the Bible say God loves us? We all can point to an obvious verse, John 3:16. "For God so loved the world that he gave his one and only Son, that whoever believes in him shall not perish but have eternal life." This verse says God loved (past tense) the world back then, but what about now? And did God love people before Jesus came? Let's find out!

Moses wrote the book of Deuteronomy, so it's been around for a while. Deuteronomy 7:8-9 says, "It was because the LORD loved you and kept the oath he swore to your ancestors that he brought you out." That's pretty straightforward. God brought the people of Israel out of slavery because He loved them. So God loved people back then.

King David and other psalmists knew that God loved them. They wrote about it a lot. Here are a couple quotes for you.

"But I trust in your unfailing love." (Psalm 13:5)

"How priceless is your unfailing love, O God!" (Psalm 36:7)

"I trust in God's unfailing love for ever and ever." (Psalm 52:8)

God's love does not fail. It never weakens or needs a break. It is always there. That's great news!

But does God still love the world? Does He still love us? Let's find out!

"But God demonstrates his own love for us in this: While we were still sinners, Christ died for us." (Romans 5:8) The fact that Christ died for us while we were still sinners proves God loves us. His love for us does not depend on our love for Him. He loved us before we loved Him (I John 4:19). And as long as people exist God will love the world. If Christ died for sinners, then He died for everyone, because everyone sins.

And check this out — "I am convinced that neither death nor life, neither angels nor demons, neither the present nor the future... will be able to separate us from the love of God that is in Christ Jesus our Lord." (Romans 8:38-39) Look at that again. Paul just said the future cannot separate us from God's love. Then God's love must extend into the future, and not just Paul's future but ours, too. That's great news!

Here's another proof for you. I John 4:8 tells us God is love. Numbers 23:19 and Psalm 55:19 say God does not change. It's reasonable to infer that God has not only ALWAYS been love, but has also always loved the world. In other words, He loved the world then and He loves the world now. In other words, yes, He still loves us. That's great news, too!

So don't let anything or anyone tell you God doesn't love you or the world anymore. That's depression or some other emotion talking. Here is the fact — "I have loved you with an everlasting love; I have drawn you with unfailing kindness. I will build you up again... you will take up your timbrels and go out to dance with the joyful." (Jeremiah 31:3 & 4)

And that's GREAT news! Make some noise!!

Today I'm going to let the sons of Korah speak to you. Check out Psalm 46 —

> "God is our refuge and strength, an ever-present help in trouble. Therefore we will not fear, though the earth give way and the mountains fall into the heart of the sea, though its waters roar and foam and the mountains quake with their surging.

> "There is a river whose streams make glad the city of God, the holy place where the Most High dwells. God is within her, she will not fall; God will help her at break of day. Nations are in uproar, kingdoms fall; he lifts his voice, the earth melts.

> "The LORD Almighty is with us; the God of Jacob is our fortress.

> "Come and see what the LORD has done, the desolations he has brought on the earth. He makes wars cease to the ends of the earth. He breaks the bow and shatters the spear; he burns the shields with fire. He says, 'Be still, and know that I am God; I will be exalted among the nations, I will be exalted in the earth.'

> "The LORD Almighty is with us; the God of Jacob is our fortress."

I'm back, with a few thoughts for you to consider. A refuge is a place you go when you need protection. The psalmists say God is our refuge, not "God can be our refuge" or "God wants to be our refuge." He is our refuge. It is a simple fact. Because of it, there's no need to fear.

The city of God is, of course, Jerusalem. We are told "God is within her." Don't forget, God is also within us. God will also help us at the break of day.

Psalm 46 talks about natural disaster and war, two things that still plague us today. We are not to fear natural disasters (verse 2) and we need to remember that God causes wars to end (verse 9). Most of all, though, we need to "be still, and know that I am God; I will be exalted among the nations, I will be exalted in the earth." (verse 10)

Verses 7 and 11 are identical. Why? For two reasons — first, it's important. "The LORD Almighty is with us; the God of Jacob is our fortress." Don't forget, a fortress is more than simply a place of refuge; it's where you find protection from the worst of the worst disasters. And the other reason is this is a song and that's the chorus.

Any songwriter will tell you the opening line is the most important line of the song. It should catch your attention and leave you wanting more. This opening line is "God is our refuge and strength, an ever-present help in trouble." I know I want to hear more, how about you? A good chorus is the second most important part of the song. It's what the songwriter wants you to remember. This chorus says "the LORD Almighty is with us; the God of Jacob is our fortress." That's worth remembering.

I need to learn this song. Let's all learn it, okay?

As a comic book fan, I've heard and taken part in discussions that other people would never consider. Questions like who is stronger, Superman or the Hulk? Who is faster, Quicksilver or the Flash? Who is the better fighter, Batman or Captain America? In short, who is the most powerful? These are fascinating questions (to the right people) with no definitive answers. We look at these amazing characters, especially in their big-budget high-tech movies, and are awestruck at what we see them do.

We tell ourselves and our kids, and maybe our grandkids, too, that God is more powerful than these superheroes. We've also seen their reaction, the expression that plainly says, "What have you been smoking?" (And sometimes we feel the same way about them.) We tell them it's true and they need to believe it, then watch them shake their heads and walk away.

At first I thought I'd talk about God's authority today, but I changed my mind. Let's look at the power of God. Can anyone truly have authority without the power to enforce it? We'll discuss God's authority next week.

First of all, God says He has power in these verses:

"And the LORD said to Abraham... 'Is anything too difficult for the LORD?'" Genesis 18:14

"And the LORD said to Moses, "Is the LORD'S power limited? Now you shall see whether My word will come true for you or not.'" Numbers 11:23

And there are many other verses that talk about the power of God. Don't forget, the Bible begins with God creating the universe, the earth and everything else out of nothing simply by saying a few words. The prophet Jeremiah said, "'Ah Lord GOD! Behold, Thou hast made the heavens and the earth by Thy great power and by Thine outstretched arm! Nothing is too difficult for Thee.'" (Jeremiah 32:17) You want to talk about power? There's power for you!

The Bible also tells us God performed many miracles to show His power. There are a lot of good examples and we all have our favorites. Perhaps the most spectacular example comes from Exodus chapters 5 through 14, the record of how God liberated the nation of Israel from Egyptian slavery. This has been the subject of several good movies, such as "The

Ten Commandments" and "Prince of Egypt," for example. The climax, watching these people walk on dry ground between two walls of water, is breathtaking and inspiring. One reason we have movie special effects is to illustrate the power of God.

Okay, I think we can agree that God has power. The obvious next question is, "Why doesn't He use it? We need some miracles, and right now!"

I agree, we could use some miracles right now. I also believe they're starting to happen (more about that later). I think that, because we've been in this fallen world as long as we have, we link power with destruction. We see explosions or disasters on the news or in movies and are awed by the devastation they cause. We also see weapons that can kill or maim dozens, hundreds or even thousands of people. That is power, yes, but it's not the only kind of power.

What takes more power, destroying something or restoring something, hurting someone or healing someone? Back in high school I tried to repair a small *Italian* motorcycle in my Auto Shop class. I fought with that thing all year and eventually gave up, saying I'd rather smash it and be done with it. I was SO glad when Dad & I finally junked it. Destroying is easy; fixing is hard!

A pastor friend of mine says God can use the coronavirus to spark a revival and is praying for it to happen. Others are asking God to spare His people, His church, and end this crisis soon. I like both ideas and am praying for both of them. Regardless of how God answers these prayers (and He will answer them), He wants to show the world His healing and restoring power. People have been destroying, hurting and killing as long as people have existed. God has been restoring, reviving and healing people just as long. He invites us to help Him and is willing to teach us how to do it. It's called loving people the way God loves us. Just like fixing something that's broken, it takes time and effort.

I'm convinced that God wants to show His power through His people. Will you let God work in you and through you to show the people around you the power of His love? That's what our country and our world needs the most.

WORD 14   Our Greatest Obsession   5-6-2020

Here's my latest encouraging word — Psalm 27, a psalm of David.

> "The LORD is my light and my salvation — whom shall I fear? The LORD is the stronghold of my life — of whom shall I be afraid?
>
> "When the wicked advance against me to devour me, it is my enemies and my foes who will stumble and fall. Though an army besiege me, my heart will not fear; though war break out against me, even then I will be confident.
>
> "One thing I ask from the LORD, this only do I seek: that I may dwell in the house of the LORD all the days of my life, to gaze on the beauty of the LORD and to seek him in his temple. For in the day of trouble he will keep me safe in his dwelling; he will hide me in the shelter of his sacred tent and set me high upon a rock.
>
> "Then my head will be exalted above the enemies who surround me; at his sacred tent I will sacrifice with shouts of joy; I will sing and make music to the LORD.
>
> "Hear my voice when I call, LORD; be merciful to me and answer me. My heart says of you, "Seek his face!" Your face, LORD, I will seek. Do not hide your face from me, do not turn your servant away in anger; you have been my helper. Do not reject me or forsake me, God my Savior. Though my father and mother forsake me, the LORD will receive me. Teach me your way, LORD; lead me in a straight path because of my oppressors. Do not turn me over to the desire of my foes, for false witnesses rise up against me, spouting malicious accusations.
>
> "I remain confident of this: I will see the goodness of the LORD in the land of the living. Wait for the LORD; be strong and take heart and wait for the LORD."

There's a lot of good stuff here, and I have a few quick thoughts for you.

Verse 1 always makes me think of Romans 8:31, because Paul & David are talking about the same thing: "If God is for us, who can be against us?" God is our light, our salvation and our stronghold. And God is for us! Because we have all that, we have NO reason to be afraid.

I'm sure you remember reading about David. He had a lot of enemies. We have our share of enemies, too, but they are a different kind of enemy. These days we face the coronavirus and other health issues, unemployment or reduced income, and more. We can and should echo David's prayer from verse 4: "One thing I ask from the LORD, this only do I seek: that I may dwell in the house of the LORD all the days of my life, to gaze on the beauty of the LORD and to seek him in his temple." It kind of sounds like an obsession, doesn't it? It's the right kind of obsession, though. An obsession doesn't have to be a bad thing; it depends on what we obsess over. God wants us to obsess over Him, like David did. Why did David want this obsession? He tells us in verse 5: "For in the day of trouble he will keep me safe in his dwelling; he will hide me in the shelter of his sacred tent and set me high upon a rock." That's one thing you can get for obsessing over God.

We are living in a day of trouble. We need God to keep us safe in His dwelling and hide us in the shelter of His sacred tent and set us high upon a rock. David said God will do that for us, as long as we are confident in His power and not afraid of our foes. Now, it's true that God can and often does protect us while we are afraid and worried. They key is to trust God while we struggle with these fears and worries. As the popular meme says, "Focus on Him, not the storm."

Let's start obsessing on Jesus Christ. Then we too can say what David did in verses 13 &14: "I remain confident of this: I will see the goodness of the LORD in the land of the living. Wait for the LORD; be strong and take heart and wait for the LORD."

WORD 15   Who's in Charge Here?   5-10-2020

It's rubber-meets-the-road time. On Thursday May 7, 2020, I found out someone at work had contracted the coronavirus. Apparently this person was not contagious when they were last at work. The company has asked that he or she (I've heard both pronouns used) stay home for another two weeks. As a result, however, the company wants us to renew our efforts to keep ourselves clean and our work areas sterilized, which is reasonable and understandable.

Naturally I was concerned and a little scared. I am... I don't want to admit this... be strong, just do it... this isn't easy... I am over 65 and, according to the CDC definition at the time, a vulnerable adult. That means my father, who is over 90 and has been living with us for the last 3 years, is even more vulnerable. One of my responsibilities as the head of the house is helping him stay healthy. I went so far as to discuss my concerns and options with HR. It all boils down to our theme for today, which is God's authority.

So what is authority? According to Dictionary.com the primary definition is, "the power to determine, adjudicate, or otherwise settle issues or disputes; jurisdiction; the right to control, command, or determine." I should also define a couple words in there we don't often use, such as adjudicate (to pronounce or decree by judicial sentence, or to settle or determine [an issue or dispute] judicially) and jurisdiction (the right, power, or authority to administer justice by hearing and determining controversies). Is that a little better?

Does the Bible say God has authority? Let's find out.

> "And Jehoshaphat stood in the assembly of Judah and Jerusalem, in the house of the LORD before the new court and said, 'O LORD God of our fathers, are you not God in heaven? You rule over all the kingdoms of the nations. In your hand are power and might, so that none is able to withstand you.'"
> (2 Chronicles 20:6)

> "God stretches the northern sky over empty space and hangs the earth on nothing. He wraps the rain in his thick clouds, and the clouds don't burst with the weight. He covers the face of the moon, shrouding it with his clouds. He created the horizon when he separated the waters: he set the boundary between

day and night. The foundations of heaven tremble; they shudder at his rebuke. By his power the sea grew calm. By his skill he crushed the great sea monster. His Spirit made the heavens beautiful, and his power pierced the gliding serpent. These are just the beginning of all that he does, merely a whisper of his power. Who, then, can comprehend the thunder of his power?" (Job 26:7-14)

"Everyone must submit to governing authorities. For all authority comes from God, and those in positions of authority have been placed there by God." (Romans 13:1)

"Jesus came to them and said, 'All authority in heaven and on earth has been given to me.'" (Matthew 28:18)

Jehoshaphat's point is that because God rules, He has authority. Job is saying that because God created everything, He also has authority over it. In Romans 13:1 the Apostle Paul said, "The authorities that exist have been established by God," meaning God is the source of authority. Jesus tells us He has been given all authority. And when we call Jesus our Lord we are saying He has power, control and authority over us. That's what "lord" means.

Okay, so God not only has authority, He is also the source of authority. Here's another important question — does He use it? Is God really in control of everything? A theologian would put it this way — is God sovereign? Let's look at some more verses.

"Many are the plans in a person's heart, but it is the LORD's purpose that prevails." (Proverbs 19:21)

"In their hearts humans plan their course, but the LORD establishes their steps." (Proverbs 16:9)

"Who can speak and have it happen if the Lord has not decreed it?" (Lamentations 3:37)

"Now listen, you who say, 'Today or tomorrow we will go to this or that city, spend a year there, carry on business and make money.' Why, you do not even know what will happen tomorrow. What is your life? You are a mist that appears for a little while and then vanishes. Instead, you ought to say, 'If it is the Lord's will, we will live and do this or that.'" (James 4:13-15)

> "In him we were also chosen, having been predestined according to the plan of him who works out everything in conformity with the purpose of his will." (Ephesians 1:11)

Let's not get sidetracked into predestination. We're not talking about that. We're talking about the One "who works out everything in conformity with the purpose of his will." That's right, everything.

One more verse on this. Jesus is speaking. "Simon, Simon, Satan has asked to sift all of you as wheat. But I have prayed for you, Simon, that your faith may not fail. And when you have turned back, strengthen your brothers." (Luke 22:31-32) This is part of what Jesus said to Simon Peter at the Last Supper. A few verses later Jesus told Peter he would deny his Lord three times. Jesus has not yet been arrested and put on trial. Jesus prayed that Peter's faith would not fail and added, "And when you have turned back, strengthen your brothers." Jesus knew Satan would attack Peter's faith and it would weaken; that's why He prayed for him. God allowed that attack because He could see the end results, that Peter's faith would return much stronger and he would strengthen his brothers.

It's starting to sound like people don't have free will, but that's not true. Here's the truth — God has the power and the creativity to take our actions, good or bad, and use them to bring about His plans. There must be times when He looks at what we've tried to do for Him and says, "That's not what I had in mind, but I can work with it."

Someone just wondered if this means God is in control of the coronavirus. The answer is simple — yes. He obviously has some purpose for it. I don't know what that purpose is, though. And the pandemic will only last as long as God wants it to. He could stop it at any time and He will stop it at the proper time. That's why I'm asking Him to end it sooner instead of later, for the sake of His people, who are caught in its effects. And the virus will touch only those He wants it to touch.

So what have I decided to do about the situation at work? I'm going to trust God and stick it out. Remember the end of the Lord's Prayer? "For thine is the kingdom and the power and the glory forever." God has the authority and the power to use it. He IS in control. That's encouraging and worthy of praise, so make some noise!

WORD 16   More Than Conquerors   5-13-2020

I haven't liked watching the news for years. I don't like bad news, and almost everything we hear is bad and frightening news, and not only about the coronavirus. These stay-at-home restrictions keep changing and were only a little bit fun when the COVID-19 crisis began. Do you have a friend or relative whose health is failing and you wish you could visit them? My wife and I do. On top of that, our economy is... not as healthy as we'd like it to be. People are nervous and scared, so here's my latest encouraging word.

I've gone over my "words" and noticed something. When I have based one on a passage of Scripture, it's been from the Old Testament. Someone is bound to wonder why I've done this. They might even wonder if I find any encouragement in the New Testament.

There definitely is encouragement in the New Testament and it's high time we read some. Let's look at one of the strongest passages now, Romans 8:31 through 39.

> "What, then, shall we say in response to these things? If God is for us, who can be against us? He who did not spare his own Son, but gave him up for us all—how will he not also, along with him, graciously give us all things? Who will bring any charge against those whom God has chosen? It is God who justifies. Who then is the one who condemns? No one. Christ Jesus who died—more than that, who was raised to life—is at the right hand of God and is also interceding for us. Who shall separate us from the love of Christ? Shall trouble or hardship or persecution or famine or nakedness or danger or sword? As it is written: 'For your sake we face death all day long; we are considered as sheep to be slaughtered.' No, in all these things we are more than conquerors through him who loved us. For I am convinced that neither death nor life, neither angels nor demons, neither the present nor the future, nor any powers, neither height nor depth, nor anything else in all creation, will be able to separate us from the love of God that is in Christ Jesus our Lord."

WOW — it doesn't get much better than that! Look at some of those statements again.

"If God is for us, who can be against us?" The obvious answer is no one. Don't forget, we're talking about the all-powerful Creator and Ruler of the universe.

"Who shall separate us from the love of Christ?" Again, no one and nothing can separate us from Christ's love. If that isn't good news, I don't know what is.

"We are more than conquerors through him who loved us." More than conquerors — that's hard for me to take in. How about you? I'm not sure I know what that means, but I do know it's a good thing.

"I am convinced that neither death nor life, neither angels nor demons, neither the present nor the future, nor any powers, neither height nor depth, nor anything else in all creation, will be able to separate us from the love of God that is in Christ Jesus our Lord." Absolutely amazing! Mind-blowing, overwhelming and every other applicable superlative we can think of!

So why are we worried about the effects of some silly little thing, like a virus or whatever little thing you're worrying about these days? The Almighty God of Heaven is on our side. Jesus died for us, He justifies us, He intercedes for us, He loves us. That makes Him is worthy of our praise, so make some noise!

Sometimes we read about God's amazing power in the Bible and think, "But that's all in the past. I don't see anything like that happening today. Something must be different now. Is God still active today?" That's an important question. The last two weeks we've looked at God's power and authority. This time we're going to explore the question "Does God still work today?"

All I can tell you is what the Bible says. It's been around a while, yes, but it is God's truth. Jesus told us God's word is truth in John 17:17. In 2 Timothy 3:16 & 17 the Apostle Paul said, "All Scripture is God-breathed and is useful for teaching, rebuking, correcting and training in righteousness, so that the servant of God may be thoroughly equipped for every good work." That's why I believe the Bible is the authoritative word of God and why I quote it to you. So here's what the Bible says on today's subject.

"And we know that in all things God works for the good of those who love him, who have been called according to his purpose." (Romans 8:28) This may be the best known verse about God's activity in our lives and it's a great one. Notice that God does not have to work for everybody's good. He works "for the good of those who love him, who have been called according to his purpose." If you have been born again, that means you.

"God has said, 'Never will I leave you; never will I forsake you.'" (Hebrews 13:5, quoting Deuteronomy 31:6) Jesus told us, "I will not leave you as orphans; I will come to you." (John 14:18) That means God is right here with each and every one of us at this very moment.

But even though you know those verses and others, and they give you some comfort, some of you aren't satisfied with that. You want proof that God is active in your life right now. That's hard for me to do, but I'll give it a try.

If the coronavirus is as contagious as we've been told, then why haven't you caught it yet? It's the middle of May 2020, maybe 10 weeks since an emergency was declared. How long can you trust only a bar of soap and disinfectants to protect you? I'm not suggesting you be stupid and throw these things away, because they can and will do some good. I'm asking how long you think common sense preventions alone can protect you.

I hurt my knee a couple weeks ago, moving some rocks that were bigger than they looked. I'm wearing a brace while I heal. Can you still walk? I've worn glasses ever since I started school as a kid. Can you see? Can you hear? I've had tinnitus, a ringing in my ears, for a long time; probably from too much loud music when I was young and stupid. There is a high pitched tone in my ears right now that does not go away. Has anything happened in your past that could have seriously affected your health or body, but didn't?

I read the obituaries in the daily paper. I'm mainly looking for my Dad's friends or people he knows, but I've seen more than that. I've seen obituaries for some friend's parents and for some of my friends, too. I see obituaries for people my age and younger every week. I don't mean to be morbid, but why are you and I still alive?

One snowy and slippery Saturday this February my wife and I were going to a memorial service for a friend. We were coming down a ramp onto a highway when we saw a car in the ditch ahead to the right. The driver ahead of us stepped on his brakes and started to slip. I tried to slow down but couldn't. I had run out of time and options. My wife cried out to Jesus for help. All we could do was watch as we sailed between those cars with mere inches of clearance on either side of us. Now I'm a careful driver, but I'm not that good. That's only one piece of personal evidence I have that proves God is actively involved in my life.

"Taste and see that the LORD is good; blessed is the one who takes refuge in him." (Psalm 34:8) Take up King David's challenge to "taste and see that the LORD is good." Take refuge in God and be blessed. Notice that blessings are not automatic; you need to take refuge in God first.

I'm reminded of something that happened in 2 Kings 6. The King of Aram had learned that God warned the prophet Elisha of the king's plans against Israel, which is why Israel kept avoiding the Arameans' efforts against them. The king decided he needed to capture Elisha and sent an army to do it. When Elisha's servant got up the next morning, he saw the army and cried out in verse 15, "Oh no, my lord! What shall we do?" Elisha tried to encourage him, but apparently it didn't work, so he prayed to God, "Open his eyes, LORD, so that he may see." Verse 17 continues, "Then the LORD opened the servant's eyes, and he looked and saw the hills full of horses and chariots of fire all around Elisha." Maybe we need our eyes opened to what God is doing around us.

Back in the day a prophet named Habakkuk asked God, "How long, LORD, must I call for help, but you do not listen?" This is how God answered him — "Look at the nations and watch— and be utterly amazed. For I am going to do something in your days that you would not believe, even if you were told." (Habakkuk 1:2 & 5) That sounds like a promise we can claim. Lord God, please do something in our days that we would not believe, even if You told us You would do it before it happened. Amaze us as only You can!

WORD 18   The Yoke's on You   5-20-2020

This week let's look at something Jesus told us in Matthew 11:28-30.

> "Come to me, all you who are weary and burdened, and I will give you rest. Take my yoke upon you and learn from me, for I am gentle and humble in heart, and you will find rest for your souls. For my yoke is easy and my burden is light."

Jesus is talking to us. We're all weary of and burdened with the COVID-19 crisis. Jesus said, "Come... and I will give you rest." That sure sounds good, doesn't it? How long has it been since you last had a truly good nights' sleep? Then keep reading, because this message is for you.

"Take my yoke upon you," Jesus said. What is He talking about? Jesus is referring to your burden, the heavy weight on your shoulders that is slowing you down and won't let you rest. He's offering a trade. He's willing to take your burden if you take up His yoke. This is better than it sounds. A yoke is built for two animals, usually oxen. One ox will be stronger than the other, but both equally share the burden. So if you take up His yoke, you are not alone with your burden. Jesus is helping you.

"Learn from me." Why? Because "I am gentle and humble in heart." Jesus wants His followers to be gentle and humble of heart, too. And isn't that what the world needs to see these days? If Jesus' followers truly are gentle and humble of heart, especially in their trials and tribulations, people would be asking us how they could become gentle and humble of heart.

"You will find rest for your souls." Did you catch that? Jesus did not say, "You might find rest for your souls" or "Some will find rest for your souls." He said all who take up His yoke WILL find rest for their souls. This is what they call a promise. This promise has a condition, though. You need to take up His yoke first. Then you find rest for your soul.

"For my yoke is easy and my burden is light." Does that mean that once we take up Christ's yoke, everything will be easy and light for us? I don't think that's what Jesus is saying. I think He's telling us He has more than enough strength for His burden. We can add our burdens to His yoke and He can carry His burden and ours, too. People and oxen have their limits, but Jesus does not.

I'm reminded of a gospel song that many singers have recorded, including Elvis Presley, called "Reach Out to Jesus," written by Ralph Carmichael. It's on YouTube. The words are great and applicable today, and Elvis does it beautifully. Reach out to Jesus, my friend, because He's reaching out to you.

WORD 19   What's in a Name?   5-24-2020

Jesus Christ is encouraging. Do I mean He is literally encouraging us right now, or that we can be encouraged by knowing who Jesus is? The simplest and best answer is yes to both questions. Today I'm going to talk about the encouragement we can get from knowing who Jesus is.

How can we know who Jesus is? How can we learn about Him? We can't sit down with Him over a cup of coffee and talk. We can't call His disciples or siblings on the phone and ask them about Him. We have to get our information indirectly, even remotely. We're getting used to doing things remotely, aren't we? We can read what His disciples wrote about Him, and they told us what He said about Himself. The Bible tells us Jesus said, "I am…" a number of times. Let's look at several of them.

> "Then Jesus declared, 'I am the bread of life. Whoever comes to me will never go hungry, and whoever believes in me will never be thirsty… I am the bread of life… Here is the bread that comes down from heaven, which anyone may eat and not die. I am the living bread that came down from heaven.'"
>
> (John 6:35, 48 & 50-51)

Jesus said "the bread of life" three times during this conversation, so it must be important. But what does it mean?

Bread may be the oldest man-made food and is considered an essential food. Most civilizations have had their own form of bread, and it is not always based on wheat. A person can live on bread and water. Jesus is saying He is as essential as bread and can sustain us, too. That's encouraging!

"When Jesus spoke again to the people, he said, 'I am the light of the world. Whoever follows me will never walk in darkness, but will have the light of life.'" (John 8:12)

Here Jesus contrasts light and darkness. Those who follow Him will not walk in darkness, so those who do not follow Him will walk in darkness. What happens when you try walking in darkness? You step on things; you bump into things and often wind up getting hurt. So Jesus wants to help us avoid the pains that can result from darkness.

What is light? From what I've read, and please remember physics is not my specialty, what we call light is a visible form of energy, which reflects off most solids into our eyes and allows us to see those objects. That's an oversimplified explanation, but I think you get the idea.

Jesus said those who follow Him will have the light of life, so He's not talking about sunlight. He's talking about the ability to see potential dangers ahead of us, things that will hurt our lives, so we can avoid them. He is willing and able to do this for us. That's encouraging!

"Jesus said again, 'Very truly I tell you, I am the gate for the sheep. All who have come before me are thieves and robbers, but the sheep have not listened to them. I am the gate; whoever enters through me will be saved.'" (John 10:7-9)

A gate can control access; it can either keep something out or in. When Jesus said, "I am the gate for the sheep," He was talking about us, His sheep, those who listened to Him instead of "thieves and robbers." Check this out — He did not say they might be saved or some will be saved. All those who entered through Him "will be saved." Now that's encouraging!

> "I am the good shepherd. The good shepherd lays down his life for the sheep. The hired hand is not the shepherd and does not own the sheep. So when he sees the wolf coming, he abandons the sheep and runs away. Then the wolf attacks the flock and scatters it. The man runs away because he is a hired hand and cares nothing for the sheep." (John 10:11-13)

Sheep need someone to watch them and care for them. They tend to wander and could easily disappear or get into trouble. And compared to other livestock animals, sheep are relatively defenseless. In Jesus' time the shepherd often owned the sheep. The owner cares for and protects the sheep. He stays with the sheep and fights off any predators that might threaten the sheep.

So Jesus is saying He will care for us, provide for us and protect us, to the point of giving His life for us. Now that's encouraging!

"Jesus said to her, 'I am the resurrection and the life. The one who believes in me will live, even though they die; and whoever lives by believing in me will never die.'" (John 11:25&26)

What is resurrection? I'm sure you have at least heard of someone who was declared dead on a hospital operating table by a medical professional, yet that person is alive now. In a literal sense they were resurrected, given life again. Jesus is saying that He not only is life, He can also give life to the dead. The gospels record some examples of that. When Jesus said someone "who believes in me will live, even though they die," He must be talking about the spiritual life He described to Nicodemus in John 3. And that's encouraging, too!

"Thomas said to him, 'Lord, we don't know where you are going, so how can we know the way?' Jesus answered, 'I am the way and the truth and the life. No one comes to the Father except through me.'" (John 14:5-6)

When Thomas asked, "How can we know the way?" what was he asking? He wanted directions. He wanted to know how to get to the place where Jesus would be. Jesus' answer was, "I am the way." If we know Him, we'll be able to find Him.

When Jesus said, "I am the truth," He wasn't talking about the facts you find in a textbook or encyclopedia. He was talking about the truth that philosophers debate, answers to the basic questions about life. He also said, "I am the life," so He should know. That's encouraging!

> "'I am the true vine, and my Father is the gardener. He cuts off every branch in me that bears no fruit, while every branch that does bear fruit he prunes so that it will be even more fruitful. You are already clean because of the word I have spoken to you. Remain in me, as I also remain in you. No branch can bear fruit by itself; it must remain in the vine. Neither can you bear fruit unless you remain in me. I am the vine; you are the branches. If you remain in me and I in you, you will bear much fruit; apart from me you can do nothing.'" (John 15:1-5)

I think we all know what a vine is, but what is a true vine? The text helps us with the answer. The true vine is the source of life for the branches. Without the true vine the branches cannot bear fruit. Verse 4 says, "No branch can bear fruit by itself; it must remain in the vine. Neither can you bear fruit unless you remain in me." We are the branches. What is the fruit, then?

There are a couple ways to answer that. There is the fruit of the Spirit from Galatians 5 — "love, joy, peace, forbearance, kindness, goodness, faithfulness, gentleness and self-control." Another form of fruit could be the people we influence for Christ. Fruit could also refer to results of the work God has given us. The best answer, however, may be to combine all these individual fruits. That's encouraging!

There's another thing to consider with these "I am" statements. When you meet someone, you usually say, "Hi, I am Joe," for example. One source I read claims these 'I am' statements use the verb that refers to names. So the Bread of Life; the Light of the World; the Gate; the Good Shepherd; the Resurrection and the Life; the Way, the Truth and the Life, and the True Vine could all be other names for Jesus Christ. And that's encouraging, too.

So when you're feeling down, remind yourself about whom Jesus is, because at that moment you will find He is VERY encouraging.

Tonight we'll look at one of my favorite psalms, Psalm 1. Here goes –

> "Blessed is the one who does not walk in step with the wicked or stand in the way that sinners take or sit in the company of mockers, but whose delight is in the law of the Lord, and who meditates on his law day and night. That person is like a tree planted by streams of water, which yields its fruit in season and whose leaf does not wither— whatever they do prospers. Not so the wicked! They are like chaff that the wind blows away. Therefore the wicked will not stand in the judgment, nor sinners in the assembly of the righteous. For the Lord watches over the way of the righteous, but the way of the wicked leads to destruction."

Psalm 1 contrasts those who are blessed and those who are not. If you want to be blessed, it starts with three things you should avoid: walking in step with the wicked, standing in the way that sinners take and sitting in the company of mockers. So what does that mean?

Walking in step with the wicked means more than simply moving at the same pace and in the same direction that the wicked walk. It means co-operating and collaborating with them. Standing in the way that sinners take does not mean blocking their progress. It means you are doing what sinners do. Sitting in the company of mockers means they are your advisors; you do what they say. And a mocker is someone who uses teasing and contemptuous language or behavior directed at a particular person or thing.

If we do those things we will NOT be blessed. Instead we need to "delight in the law of the Lord and meditate on His law day and night." That's how we become blessed.

That blessed person "is like a tree planted by streams of water, which yields its fruit in season and whose leaf does not wither." In other words, whatever this blessed person does prospers. A tree planted by streams of water always has what it needs to grow and it grows well. It yields its fruit in season and its leaves do not wither. God wants to provide for us and help us grow in exactly that way. He wants us to prosper, grow strong and produce good fruit.

The wicked, however, are not blessed and do not prosper. They are like chaff, which is the dry, scaly protective casing of the seeds of cereal grains, which needs to be separated from the grain by winnowing or threshing. It's a waste product, useless and worthless. In Matthew 3:12 John the Baptist said this about Jesus, "His winnowing fork is in his hand, and he will clear his threshing floor, gathering his wheat into the barn and burning up the chaff with unquenchable fire." That's why the wicked cannot stand at God's judgment. And sinners cannot stand in the assembly of the righteous because they are not righteous.

When verse 6 says, "the Lord watches over the way of the righteous," it does not mean God simply observes righteous people as they work at being righteous. It means He is actively guiding them into righteousness, kind of like that tree planted by streams of water. The psalmist makes a contrast here between the way of the righteous and the way of the wicked. We are told "the way of the wicked leads to destruction." So the way of the righteous should lead to something good, and it does. Earlier we were told the righteous will prosper.

Prosperity is not a solid economy. It's not a humongous bank account, either. Prosperity is recognizing the abundance God has given us. In Philippians 4:11 Paul said, "I have learned to be content whatever the circumstances." Even in our weakened economy we still have more than most inhabitants of third world countries. We can be thankful for that and praise God for it.

I'll admit it. I'm in shock. Things like the death of George Floyd on Monday May 25, 2020, and its aftermath are not supposed to happen in your home town. The overwhelming reaction to all of it is bad enough. Rioting, fires, buildings destroyed and more. The images I've seen are terrible and frightening, because I know the area. I've been there many times. I live in a suburb of Minneapolis MN.

This hurts, yes, but I know my pain isn't anything like those who have lost their business or the neighborhood grocery store. I cannot imagine what they are going through. Those people aren't unique in their pain, either. People across the country and throughout history have had to deal with losing their means of support or their possessions or both. Please don't misunderstand me. I'm not trying to minimize anyone's pain. I'm simply saying that pain like theirs has been with us for a long time.

This devastation also had a secondary effect for me. See, my favorite bookstore, the oldest and one of the last of its kind in the country, was about a block and a half north of Lake Street on Chicago Avenue, maybe a half hour drive from my home. It was an elite bookstore and internationally known. I've been told that people from Europe would come to New York and decide that, as long as they're in the country, they'd fly a couple more hours to Minneapolis and visit Uncle Hugo's. It was torched Friday night May 29, 2020. Before I started writing I saw a picture of the building, or what's left of it — a pile of rubble. The article accompanying that picture said the owner doesn't know if his insurance will cover the damages or not. We have literally lost a national treasure and I am in mourning from this double gut punch.

Some of you are thinking, "The only reason you feel anything right now is that this store was one of the places where you could feed your geek. Man up, you'll get over it." To that I say two things. One, you're not listening to me. You don't know what you're talking about. And two, believe it or not, I am in mourning. Let me grieve. I can't move on until I finish.

Let's look at how some people in the Bible dealt with extreme emotional pain, far worse than mine. That should help all of us.

One person in particular comes to mind. We are told, "This man was blameless and upright; he feared God and shunned evil. He had seven sons and three daughters, and he owned seven thousand sheep, three thousand camels, five hundred yoke of oxen and five hundred donkeys, and had a large number of servants. He was the greatest man among all the people of the East." His name was Job. Through no fault of his, it was all taken away — family, livestock, everything. A little later, Job lost his health. He had "painful sores from the soles of his feet to the crown of his head" (2:7). Through all this "Job did not sin in what he said" (2:10).

This went on for a while. We know three friends came and mourned with him for a week (2:11-13). Job then did some honest and understandable whining (3:1-26), and they gave him bad advice (chapters 4-37) because they did not understand his situation.

You see, Job's friends insisted that his affliction was his fault; God was reacting to something Job did or should have done. Job insisted he had done nothing to deserve this treatment; he was innocent and only wanted justice. His friends couldn't believe that and kept telling him to search his heart and confess his evil ways. In a nutshell Job basically told them, "You guys don't know what you're talking about."

Here is one thing Job said that summarizes his position —

> "If only I knew where to find [God]; if only I could go to his dwelling! I would state my case before him and fill my mouth with arguments. I would find out what he would answer me, and consider what he would say to me... But he knows the way that I take; when he has tested me, I will come forth as gold. My feet have closely followed his steps; I have kept to his way without turning aside. I have not departed from the commands of his lips; I have treasured the words of his mouth more than my daily bread." (23:3-5, 10-12).

Does this sound at all familiar? Have you ever said or heard anyone say something like "Sit down, God, we need to talk"? That's what Job is doing, and that's not a bad thing. It helps us understand what we feel and get it out into the open. We have to acknowledge what we are going through before God can help us deal with it. And God did help Job deal with his losses and his thoughtless friends.

God's answer in Job chapters 38 through 41 boils down to "I know and can do SO many things you cannot. You are not my equal. You are nothing like me. How can you presume to judge me?"

"How can you presume to judge me?" We hear that a lot from the people around us. It's a valid point. How can we judge someone else when we know so little about them or have so little in common? And who are we to judge?

In chapter 42 Job realized he wanted to judge God for His actions, but found out he could not because God is so much more than we are. His early attitude was far better — "The LORD gave and the LORD has taken away; may the name of the LORD be praised" (1:21) and "Shall we accept good from God, and not trouble?" (2:10) Job repented of his bad attitude (42:6) and God forgave him.

And how did things work out for Job? Check this out —

> "The Lord blessed the latter part of Job's life more than the former part. He had fourteen thousand sheep, six thousand camels, a thousand yoke of oxen and a thousand donkeys. And he also had seven sons and three daughters... After this, Job lived a hundred and forty years; he saw his children and their children to the fourth generation. And so Job died, an old man and full of years." (Job 42:12-13, 16-17)

His wealth was doubled and he had another family!

The whole point of the book of Job is that the powerful yet unfamiliar God we serve always has a reason for what He does. We may not see it, and we won't understand it while we're going through it, but that doesn't mean there is no reason for what happened.

Let's look at another case, but we'll do it next time. This is long enough the way it is.

[Author's note — this "word" and the next were written together, but were posted separately due to their size.]

On Sunday we saw the lesson God taught Job (and us), remember? Today let's look at another case, this time concerning a group of oppressed people. It's well documented in the Bible, so we'll get a good description of the events.

According to 2 Kings 24 & 25 the Babylonian King Nebuchadnezzar wanted to conquer Israel and captured several of their kings, but Israel kept rebelling against him. Eventually King Nebuchadnezzar put Jerusalem under siege, captured it, burned down its important buildings and deported all its leaders to Babylon. Even though some Israelites were still working their land around Jerusalem, Israel became a broken and divided nation.

As you can imagine, the whole process was painful for the Israelites. The prophet Habakkuk complained to God about their situation in the first chapter of his book and he could be talking about the events surrounding the death of George Floyd in Minneapolis.

> "How long, LORD, must I call for help, but you do not listen? Or cry out to you, 'Violence!' but you do not save? Why do you make me look at injustice? Why do you tolerate wrongdoing? Destruction and violence are before me; there is strife, and conflict abounds. Therefore the law is paralyzed, and justice never prevails. The wicked hem in the righteous, so that justice is perverted."   (Habakkuk 1:2-4)

This is God's answer: "Look at the nations and watch— and be utterly amazed. For I am going to do something in your days that you would not believe, even if you were told. I am raising up the Babylonians, that ruthless and impetuous people, who sweep across the whole earth to seize dwellings not their own" (Hab 1:5-6). So God wanted Babylon to conquer Israel? That's what He said, and it happened exactly as He said it would.

Around the same time God told the prophet Jeremiah,

> "'I will summon all the peoples of the north and my servant Nebuchadnezzar king of Babylon,' declares the Lord, 'and I will bring them against this land and its inhabitants and against all the surrounding nations... these nations will serve the king of Babylon seventy years. But when the seventy years are fulfilled, I will punish the king of Babylon and his nation, the land of the

Babylonians, for their guilt,' declares the Lord, 'and will make it desolate forever.'"   (Jeremiah 25:9, 11-12)

2 Kings 24:18-20 tell us why it had to happen. "Zedekiah... did evil in the eyes of the LORD, just as Jehoiakim had done. It was because of the LORD's anger that all this happened to Jerusalem and Judah, and in the end He thrust them from His presence."

Those 70 years ended when another king of Babylon (Persia) gave this decree:

> "The LORD, the God of heaven, has given me all the kingdoms of the earth and He has appointed me to build a temple for Him at Jerusalem in Judah. Any of His people among you may go up to Jerusalem in Judah and build the temple of the LORD, the God of Israel, the God who is in Jerusalem, and may their God be with them. And in any locality where survivors may now be living, the people are to provide them with silver and gold, with goods and livestock, and with freewill offerings for the temple of God in Jerusalem."   (Ezra 1:2-4)

The Babylonian captivity was finally over! The books of Ezra and Nehemiah record the rebuilding and resettling of Jerusalem.

God had a plan and He told Jeremiah about it when He put His plan in motion. The people who were paying attention knew how long this exile would last, but they had to be patient until the plan was complete.

The point is that, even though God has a plan, it's going to take time for it to happen and whining about it won't change anything.

People were looking at the George Floyd case and saying, "This is not justice," just like Habakkuk did, and they're right. Will we see justice? Yes, but it could take a while. Many people want to do something, and that's good, but is what they want truly justice? The Bible tells us in two places (Romans 12:19 and Deuteronomy 32:35) that vengeance belongs to God, not people. We need to vent or purge our emotions somehow, yes, but in a positive and non-violent way.

Many people are calling for unity. I agree with that, but I don't think it's enough. I think we need to repent, as Job did, and admit that the Almighty

God of the universe not only has a plan, but is also working to bring about His goals for it.

Someone just said, "Wait a minute. I thought this was supposed to be encouraging." It is, when you put everything together. God is in control, even of these uncertain times, and that's encouraging. He has a plan and it's encouraging to know that, too. He has also promised to be with us throughout the difficulties we will face while His plan is in action and bless us as we obey Him, and that's VERY encouraging. He may ask that we do something difficult, meaning patiently wait for His plan to work out, but only because it's the best thing we can do. We need to believe that the same powerful God who answered Job and set a time limit on the Babylonian exile will work out His solution.

And how am I doing? I'm much better, thanks. Writing out my thoughts and feelings, and clarifying them, helps me work through them. I'll always be sad that Uncle Hugo's is gone, but I'm done mourning. God is in control and He has a plan, you know?

[Author's note: After a number of setbacks, Uncle Hugo's Science Fiction Bookstore reopened August 14, 2022, at reduced hours in a different part of Minneapolis. They resumed normal hours on September 6, 2022, about three weeks later. And yes, that makes me VERY happy.]

When I sat down to my computer today I thought I had a good topic, but another idea hit me right between the eyes: what does the Bible say about justice? In the light of the events of the summer of 2020, that seems quite appropriate, don't you think?

First of all, what is justice? According to Dictionary.com, justice could mean one of three things:

> "1) The quality of being just; righteousness, equitableness, or moral rightness [for example, to uphold the justice of a cause]. 2) Rightfulness or lawfulness, as of a claim or title; justness of ground or reason [for example, to complain with justice]. 3) The moral principle determining just conduct."

That begs the question, what does being just mean? Dictionary.com gives four answers, depending on how it's used:

> "1) Guided by truth, reason, justice, and fairness [for example, "We hope to be just in our understanding of such difficult situations"]. 2) Done or made according to principle; equitable; proper [for example, a just reply]. 3) Based on right; rightful; lawful: [for example, a just claim]. 4) In keeping with truth or fact; true; correct [for example, a just analysis]."

Does the Bible agree with this? Yes, it does, according to the following verses.

"He has shown you, O mortal, what is good. And what does the LORD require of you? To act justly and to love mercy and to walk humbly with your God." (Micah 6:8)

"This is what the Lord says: 'Maintain justice and do what is right, for my salvation is close at hand and my righteousness will soon be revealed.'" (Isaiah 56:1)

"Speak up and judge fairly; defend the rights of the poor and needy." (Proverbs 31:9)

"And will not God bring about justice for his chosen ones, who cry out to him day and night? Will he keep putting them off? I tell you, he will see that they get justice, and quickly." (Luke 18:7-8)

And that is only the beginning. Ask Google "what does the Bible say about justice?" and check out the results. Don't forget, though, that the Bible is all about relationships; mainly about how we relate to God, but also about how we relate to other people. Doing what is right is important, but getting right with God needs to come first.

Okay, the Bible tells us God is just and we should be, too. Does it say anything about prejudice?

The word prejudice is not in the Bible, but that doesn't mean the Bible doesn't talk about prejudice. The account of Moses and the liberation of Israel from Egypt (Exodus 4 through 14) is obviously against slavery. The time that Jesus met the Samaritan woman at the well in John 4:4-42 is very relevant.

After Jesus asked her for a drink "the Samaritan woman said to him, 'You are a Jew and I am a Samaritan woman. How can you ask me for a drink?' (For Jews do not associate with Samaritans.)" (John 4:9) Why didn't Jews associate with Samaritans? That's a long and involved story. I'll summarize it by saying there were several social, political and religious reasons. And it wasn't a polite disagreement, either. There was genuine hatred between Jews and Samaritans. That sounds like it came out of today's newspaper, doesn't it?

According to John 4:8, Jesus was alone because his disciples had gone to buy food. When they returned in verse 27, they "were surprised to find him talking with a woman." Notice that the verse simply says "a woman," not "a Samaritan woman." Women were second-class citizens at the time and on top of that, this was a Samaritan woman; in that place and time she had a lot going against her. That didn't matter to Jesus, though. To Him, she was simply someone who needed to hear the truth, so He told her the truth.

That's only one place where the Bible talks about prejudice. There are others, but I think you see the point. God is against prejudice. John 3:16 says He loves the entire world.

I feel I should end this with a challenge, a call to not only commit ourselves to justice, but also to cast off our prejudices. That would be a good and even a necessary thing, but it's not the purpose for these writings. I want to encourage people, to give hope and purpose in these uncertain days. So I'm going to try something here...

What kind of a world do you want to live in? If you're like me (I know that thought scares you, but bear with me here), you want a world where ALL people are wanted and loved, treated fairly and with respect, and have equal opportunities and freedoms, regardless of their color, their beliefs, their background and their gender. (There, that's not weird at all, right?)

Here's the encouragement — that's the kind of world God wants, too. Even though our world is broken and twisted, God is willing give it another chance and, eventually, repair it.

And here's the challenge — He needs us to help build that world. Jesus left His followers here to show the world that He makes a difference in our lives.

So what do we do? I could give you some general answers, but that really won't help. You'll have to ask God what you need to do. He will answer, and that's encouraging, too — not only for you, but for the people whose lives you will affect.

Here's my latest encouraging word, this time Jesus' encouraging words, from Matthew chapter 6.

> "I tell you, do not worry about your life, what you will eat or drink; or about your body, what you will wear. Is not life more than food, and the body more than clothes? Look at the birds of the air; they do not sow or reap or store away in barns, and yet your heavenly Father feeds them. Are you not much more valuable than they? Can any one of you by worrying add a single hour to your life? And why do you worry about clothes? See how the flowers of the field grow. They do not labor or spin. Yet I tell you that not even Solomon in all his splendor was dressed like one of these. If that is how God clothes the grass of the field, which is here today and tomorrow is thrown into the fire, will he not much more clothe you—you of little faith? So do not worry, saying, 'What shall we eat?' or 'What shall we drink?' or 'What shall we wear?' For the pagans run after all these things, and your heavenly Father knows that you need them. But seek first his kingdom and his righteousness, and all these things will be given to you as well. Therefore do not worry about tomorrow, for tomorrow will worry about itself. Each day has enough trouble of its own."   (Matthew 6:25-34)

That's all I'm going to say today. There is a time and a place for in-depth Bible study and we can learn a lot from the great articles and books written by many wise and highly educated people. But remember who Jesus was talking to: fishermen, carpenters and farmers — common working people like you and me. He's happy if you get His main point, because a lot of people didn't. Don't forget, it's the simple truth of the Gospel that can change the world. Now that's an encouraging thought, and it makes the verses I quoted above encouraging, too!

Before I sat down to my computer to write, I started a YouTube video of instrumental hymns, so my family could listen after church. Just now it was playing "Nearer My God to Thee." Let's all draw closer to God for the next few minutes and see how 1 Corinthians 13 can encourage us.

> "If I speak in the tongues of men or of angels, but do not have love, I am only a resounding gong or a clanging cymbal. If I have the gift of prophecy and can fathom all mysteries and all knowledge, and if I have a faith that can move mountains, but do not have love, I am nothing. If I give all I possess to the poor and give over my body to hardship that I may boast, but do not have love, I gain nothing.

> "Love is patient, love is kind. It does not envy, it does not boast, it is not proud. It does not dishonor others, it is not self-seeking, it is not easily angered, it keeps no record of wrongs. Love does not delight in evil but rejoices with the truth. It always protects, always trusts, always hopes, always perseveres.

> "Love never fails. But where there are prophecies, they will cease; where there are tongues, they will be stilled; where there is knowledge, it will pass away. For we know in part and we prophesy in part, but when completeness comes, what is in part disappears. When I was a child, I talked like a child, I thought like a child, I reasoned like a child. When I became a man, I put the ways of childhood behind me. For now we see only a reflection as in a mirror; then we shall see face to face. Now I know in part; then I shall know fully, even as I am fully known.

> "And now these three remain: faith, hope and love. But the greatest of these is love."

These verses are often quoted at weddings, which is good. You need this kind of love to have a good marriage. But the apostle Paul was not talking only about marriage, he was talking about life. We need this kind of love in order to have good relationships with other people, and not just the people in our neighborhoods, but also the people on the other side of the country or even the other side of the planet.

I think that is what this [2020] summer's rioting is about. I think the rioters are saying they are not getting the love they should. When someone says, "Black lives matter," they mean, "What happens to me should matter to you. I should matter to you." They are right. That's important, but it's only part of that they truly need. Love is more than showing someone else that they matter to you; it's also showing them that they matter to God. Don't forget, John 3:16 says God loves the whole world. Only God can truly change the world, but He expects us to help. We all have a part to play.

Let's read verses 4 through 7 of 1 Corinthians 13 again:

> "Love is patient, love is kind. It does not envy, it does not boast, it is not proud. It does not dishonor others, it is not self-seeking, it is not easily angered, it keeps no record of wrongs. Love does not delight in evil but rejoices with the truth. It always protects, always trusts, always hopes, always perseveres."

I'm reminded of Matthew 7:12, "So in everything, do to others what you would have them do to you, for this sums up the Law and the Prophets." Isn't that how you would like your spouse or a co-worker or a police officer to treat you? Patience, kindness, humility, honoring and protecting others — Galatians 5:22 tells us that this kind of love comes from the Spirit of God.

I Corinthians 13:10 is the key to the last paragraph: "When completeness comes, what is in part disappears." Paul is talking about a transition, a change, and compares it to becoming an adult (verse 11). When that change is complete, prophecies will cease, tongues will be stilled and knowledge will pass away (verse 8). That's when we shall see face to face and shall know fully, even as we are fully known (verse 12). Let's not ask, "What is this change?" right now, because that would take us away from Paul's point, which is that love never fails (verse 8) even though other things may change.

1 Corinthians 13:13 says, "And now these three remain: faith, hope and love. But the greatest of these is love." Over the last 12 weeks I've tried to encourage your faith and give you hope. Today I want to encourage you to love everyone around you the way Jesus loved everyone around Him. A lot of people talk about changing the world. Loving people the way Jesus loved them WILL change the world, because that's what happened

2000 years ago. Nothing in this world is more radical or more desperately needed.

So let's be world-changers and encouragers. Show Jesus' love to at least one other person today.

Here is another of my favorites, Psalm 103.

> "Praise the LORD, my soul; all my inmost being, praise his holy name. Praise the LORD, my soul, and forget not all his benefits— who forgives all your sins and heals all your diseases, who redeems your life from the pit and crowns you with love and compassion, who satisfies your desires with good things so that your youth is renewed like the eagle's.

> "The LORD works righteousness and justice for all the oppressed. He made known his ways to Moses, his deeds to the people of Israel: The LORD is compassionate and gracious, slow to anger, abounding in love. He will not always accuse, nor will he harbor his anger forever; he does not treat us as our sins deserve or repay us according to our iniquities. For as high as the heavens are above the earth, so great is his love for those who fear him; as far as the east is from the west, so far has he removed our transgressions from us.

> "As a father has compassion on his children, so the LORD has compassion on those who fear him; for he knows how we are formed, he remembers that we are dust. The life of mortals is like grass, they flourish like a flower of the field; the wind blows over it and it is gone, and its place remembers it no more. But from everlasting to everlasting the LORD's love is with those who fear him, and his righteousness with their children's children— with those who keep his covenant and remember to obey his precepts. The LORD has established his throne in heaven, and his kingdom rules over all.

> "Praise the LORD, you his angels, you mighty ones who do his bidding, who obey his word. Praise the LORD, all his heavenly hosts, you his servants who do his will. Praise the LORD, all his works everywhere in his dominion. Praise the LORD, my soul."

Yes, praise the Lord, my friends! Look at those benefits again — "who forgives all your sins and heals all your diseases, who redeems your life from the pit and crowns you with love and compassion, who satisfies your desires with good things so that your youth is renewed like the eagle's."

That's better than your benefits package at work, right?

Verses 11 & 12 are among my all time favorites — "For as high as the heavens are above the earth, so great is his love for those who fear him; as far as the east is from the west, so far has he removed our transgressions from us." Every time I read them I'm encouraged by the reminder of God's immense love and forgiveness. It blows my puny human mind.

And David speaks of puny humans, too, in verses 13 through 16. God knows our limitations, that we are made of dust and as short lived as grass, and allows for them. Verse 17 reminds us, "from everlasting to everlasting the LORD's love is with those who fear him, and his righteousness with their children's children—with those who keep his covenant and remember to obey his precepts. The LORD has established his throne in heaven, and his kingdom rules over all." That's amazing! His love is with those who fear him, and His righteousness is with their children's children. All they need to do is keep his covenant and remember to obey his precepts.

And why does God do all this? The foundation for this extravagance is in verse 19 — "The LORD has established his throne in heaven, and his kingdom rules over all." In other words, God not only rules over everything, He literally is over everything because His throne is in Heaven.

Is that encouraging or what? Make your noise – praise God!!

WORD 27   Victory is SO Close   6-21-2020

I've liked 1 Corinthians 15 for a long time. Once I wanted to memorize it; maybe it's time to try again. The closing verses are especially meaningful to me.

> "I declare to you, brothers and sisters, that flesh and blood cannot inherit the kingdom of God, nor does the perishable inherit the imperishable. Listen, I tell you a mystery: We will not all sleep, but we will all be changed— in a flash, in the twinkling of an eye, at the last trumpet. For the trumpet will sound, the dead will be raised imperishable, and we will be changed. For the perishable must clothe itself with the imperishable, and the mortal with immortality. When the perishable has been clothed with the imperishable, and the mortal with immortality, then the saying that is written will come true: 'Death has been swallowed up in victory.'
>
> "'Where, O death, is your victory? Where, O death, is your sting?'
>
> "The sting of death is sin, and the power of sin is the law. But thanks be to God! He gives us the victory through our Lord Jesus Christ.
>
> "Therefore, my dear brothers and sisters, stand firm. Let nothing move you. Always give yourselves fully to the work of the Lord, because you know that your labor in the Lord is not in vain."
>
> (I Cor. 15:50-58)

We hear a lot of talk about "the new normal." It means that we've gone through a major or fundamental change, a paradigm shift. It's sudden and demanding, and we must accept and adjust to the fact that life will never be the same, because no one on earth can undo what has been done. Both the novel coronavirus and the backlash from the death of George Floyd are forcing the world to alter its behavior in many ways.

That kind of change is exactly what Paul is talking about here. A believer's life does not truly end with death. Instead, it is a change, a new beginning when God gives us victory over the sting of death and the power of sin through the resurrection of our Lord and Savior Jesus Christ!

That in itself is incredible news, the last of an impressive string of teachings (read the chapter), but what blows me away is Paul's conclusion: stand firm; let nothing move you, because we know that our labor in the Lord is not in vain, because of the victory we have over sin and death through Jesus Christ. In other words, nothing that happens to you in this temporary and perishable world, not even death itself, changes your God-given mission, so stick with it.

I know people who feel we need to simply endure the events going on in the world around us, because God will let it will wash over us with all the power and effectiveness of gentle waves at the beach. There is some truth to that, but it's not what Paul means by "stand firm." He wants us to get off our beach towels and get back to the Lord's work! He's saying the affairs of this world are temporary, perishable, mortal and we need to be about the eternal, imperishable and immortal work of the Lord.

So be encouraged! The things of this world may damage our bodies, but God says those bodies will be changed, they aren't meant to last forever. We may even find our lives endangered, but that simply means we can go to be with Jesus. No matter what happens to us, God has given us the victory through our Lord Jesus Christ, just like He gave the nation of Israel victory over their enemies so many times in the Old Testament. That is incredible news — make some noise and praise God!!

WORD 28   Encouraging and Challenging   6-24-2020

It's cool and fascinating that the Bible can be both encouraging and challenging at the same time. I'm sure you've seen that before, too. Let's look at one time the Apostle John does it.

> "Dear friends, let us love one another, for love comes from God. Everyone who loves has been born of God and knows God. Whoever does not love does not know God, because God is love. This is how God showed his love among us: He sent his one and only Son into the world that we might live through him. This is love: not that we loved God, but that he loved us and sent his Son as an atoning sacrifice for our sins. Dear friends, since God so loved us, we also ought to love one another. No one has ever seen God; but if we love one another, God lives in us and his love is made complete in us.

> "This is how we know that we live in him and he in us: He has given us of his Spirit. And we have seen and testify that the Father has sent his Son to be the Savior of the world. If anyone acknowledges that Jesus is the Son of God, God lives in them and they in God. And so we know and rely on the love God has for us.

> "God is love. Whoever lives in love lives in God, and God in them. This is how love is made complete among us so that we will have confidence on the day of judgment: In this world we are like Jesus. There is no fear in love. But perfect love drives out fear, because fear has to do with punishment. The one who fears is not made perfect in love.

> "We love because he first loved us. Whoever claims to love God yet hates a brother or sister is a liar. For whoever does not love their brother and sister, whom they have seen, cannot love God, whom they have not seen. And he has given us this command: Anyone who loves God must also love their brother and sister."
>
> (I John 4:7-21)

Read that again; soak in it for a while. There's so much good stuff in here, it's hard to know what to emphasize. John has been called the apostle of love, because he talks about love quite a bit. This passage is no exception.

Here's the encouragement: God is love. He loved us and sent his Son as an atoning sacrifice for our sins. He sent his Son to be the Savior of the world. God lives in us through His love.

And here's the challenge: "Whoever claims to love God yet hates a brother or sister is a liar. For whoever does not love their brother and sister, whom they have seen, cannot love God, whom they have not seen. And he has given us this command: Anyone who loves God must also love their brother and sister." (verses 20-21) "Whoever does not love does not know God." (verse 8) If someone is a brother or sister in the Lord, we are to love them regardless of color or class. And don't forget verse 18: "There is no fear in love. But perfect love drives out fear, because fear has to do with punishment. The one who fears is not made perfect in love."

We've been told again and again that black lives matter. That's true, but there's more to it. The whole truth is that ALL lives matter to God, and they should matter to us, too. Let's all decide to love all our brothers and sisters in the Lord.

WORD 29   Let's Be Like Jesus   6-28-2020

The men's Bible study I attend has taken the summer off, because several of the guys often take vacations during the summer. That may not be true this year (2020), but we're still taking the summer off. At times like this I usually turn to the Gospels for my Bible reading. I want to be more like Jesus, so I keep reading about Him, thinking it will eventually rub off on me, you know? Let's look at what Jesus said in John 14:23-29.

> "Anyone who loves me will obey my teaching. My Father will love them, and we will come to them and make our home with them. Anyone who does not love me will not obey my teaching. These words you hear are not my own; they belong to the Father who sent me.

> "All this I have spoken while still with you. But the Advocate, the Holy Spirit, whom the Father will send in my name, will teach you all things and will remind you of everything I have said to you. Peace I leave with you; my peace I give you. I do not give to you as the world gives. Do not let your hearts be troubled and do not be afraid.

> "You heard me say, 'I am going away and I am coming back to you.' If you loved me, you would be glad that I am going to the Father, for the Father is greater than I. I have told you now before it happens, so that when it does happen you will believe."

Jesus taught us what the Father told Him to say. The people who don't love Him will not obey His teaching. Not only does the Father love us when we obey that teaching, He and Jesus also come to live with us. And the Holy Spirit comes, too, to teach us all things and remind us of every-thing Jesus said to us through the Bible.

There is so much turmoil around us these days. Demonstrating doesn't seem to be enough, people are looting and rioting and pulling down stat-ues and more. The peace Jesus leaves us doesn't simply mean a friendly lack of violence. He's talking about a calming awareness that God is with us, in control and on our side, even while the neighborhood is burning and crumbling around us. That's the peace we need, and we need to show it to the world.

Going Viral – Encouraging Words for Discouraging Times   67

Jesus is with the Father now, and we should be glad about that, but He promised to come back. He told us He was going away before He left, so we would believe Him when it happened. But believe what? In verse 28 He said, "I am going away and I am coming back to you." That's what we need to believe, that He is coming back! God has not given up on this world. He has plans for it and no matter what people do, those plans will come to pass. As the saying goes, you can take it to the bank. That's encouraging!!

Did you have a good Fourth of July? We have a lot to celebrate! We have so many freedoms, rights and privileges in the USA. These days I prefer to celebrate and watch fireworks inside, to prevent insects from feasting on my body. Last night and for many years we've watched a great PBS special that is broadcast from Washington DC. I highly recommend it for others like me who attract mosquitoes better than a magnet attracts iron filings. But I digress...

Let's look at Psalm 40 today. I'm not going to quote the whole psalm, so I can make some comments and still keep this "word" to a manageable size.

> "I waited patiently for the Lord; he turned to me and heard my cry. He lifted me out of the slimy pit, out of the mud and mire; he set my feet on a rock and gave me a firm place to stand. He put a new song in my mouth, a hymn of praise to our God. Many will see and fear the Lord and put their trust in him.

> "Blessed is the one who trusts in the Lord, who does not look to the proud, to those who turn aside to false gods. Many, Lord my God, are the wonders you have done, the things you planned for us. None can compare with you; were I to speak and tell of your deeds, they would be too many to declare.

> "Sacrifice and offering you did not desire— but my ears you have opened— burnt offerings and sin offerings you did not require. Then I said, 'Here I am, I have come— it is written about me in the scroll. I desire to do your will, my God; your law is within my heart.'

> "I proclaim your saving acts in the great assembly; I do not seal my lips, Lord, as you know. I do not hide your righteousness in my heart; I speak of your faithfulness and your saving help. I do not conceal your love and your faithfulness from the great assembly.

> "Do not withhold your mercy from me, Lord; may your love and faithfulness always protect me. For troubles without number surround me; my sins have overtaken me, and I cannot see. They are more than the hairs of my head, and my heart fails

within me. Be pleased to save me, Lord; come quickly, Lord, to help me… may all who seek you rejoice and be glad in you; may those who long for your saving help always say, 'The LORD is great!'

"But as for me, I am poor and needy; may the Lord think of me. You are my help and my deliverer; you are my God, do not delay."

We also need to wait patiently for the Lord. He does hear our cries, you know. "For the eyes of the Lord are on the righteous and his ears are attentive to their prayer." (1 Peter 3:12) "And if we know that he hears us—whatever we ask—we know that we have what we asked of him." (1 John 5:15)

Remember all the wonderful things God has already done for you in the past and tell people about them, as David did in Psalm 40 and others. That does not mean we need to ingratiate ourselves to God; He doesn't play favorites and He can tell when we're not sincere. David is saying we need to be openly grateful for every blessing God has given to us, because that sort of thing makes God happy.

We all need God's mercy, love and faithfulness. We also are poor and needy with innumerable troubles, are overwhelmed by our sins, and desperately need God's help and salvation. David very much needed the assurance we have that God would deliver him from his troubles and his sins. "Everyone who calls on the name of the Lord will be saved." (Joel 2:32, quoted in Acts 2:21and Romans 10:13) Yes, God will deliver us, and that's VERY encouraging.

2020 has been an unusual year for Wonder Ministries. If you don't know what I'm talking about, stop reading right now and check out www.wonder-ministries.com. I'll wait here until you come back.

On the third weekend of May I normally have a table for Christian comic books and sponsor a Chapel service and panel discussion at a local comic book convention. In late March or early April I learned that this show was canceled. Just the other night I learned they had canceled their October show, too. I had been looking forward to it, but I can't be too disappointed and here's why.

About a year and a half ago the Youth Pastor for the church I attend left for another position. He and his wife had been living in the old parsonage. Now it was vacant and the church was wondering what we should do about that. Maybe two months later a missionary family with 6 young boys came back to Minnesota from Chad when they learned their youngest son needed a liver transplant and urgent medical care. They needed a place to live relatively close to the hospital in Minneapolis, so the church told them they could stay in the old parsonage. It sounded like a good solution and the situation worked out rather well for everybody.

About a month ago, after much medical care and many trips to the hospital, this little boy was reasonably stable and his Dad accepted a call to pastor a local church. I had been thinking of doing something for this family for a while and realized that the time had come, so I packaged up an Action Bible along with a couple of free comics and gave it to them, along with a summary of my work with Christian comics for the father.

Sunday July 5, 2020, was my second Sunday back to church after the Governor of Minnesota allowed them to re-open at limited capacity. When I checked our church mail box I found a little envelope. It was a thank you card for the comic books from the family. A thank you card always makes you feel good, but this one was special. You see, one of the boys wrote his own message on the outside of the envelope: "I really liked the Bible and I keep reading it. I'm 8 years old."

Even though Wonder Ministries is and has been trying to reach out to local churches, my main work right now is in the local comic book conventions, and we all know there were no large public gatherings in 2020. It's true I needed a break and I had plenty to do at home, but this work is my calling and I missed it! I have missed seeing the people I've come to know at these shows, as well as the contact with comic book fans both Christian and not. In other words, I wasn't convinced I was serving God exactly the way He wanted me to serve Him.

Then I saw that thank you card. Thanks, Joe; you made my summer! I felt a familiar thrill when I heard you were regularly reading the Action Bible. I'm used to getting that feeling at comic book shows after Mom or Dad buy something for their child and the kid is pulling it out of the bag as they walk away to check it out one more time – the feeling that God is at work here and I am blessed to be a part of it. I was VERY encouraged and recharged by your simple thank you. It helped me realize that God is still trying to work through me, even when He's given me a break. It also makes me wonder what other surprises God has in store for me this year...

WORD 32   Can We Make God Happy?   7-19-2020

A very interesting thought occurred to me as I wrapped up the July 5 word and I thought it might be a good one for us to explore today. Here is that thought — if you knew you could do something that would make God happy, would you do it?

Let's start by thinking about what the question means. Do our actions affect God? Assuming God has emotions, can we influence them enough to make Him happy or sad or angry?

The well known verse John 3:16 says God loves the world. Genesis 6:6 tells us, "The LORD regretted that he had made human beings on the earth, and his heart was deeply troubled." King David knew about God's emotions. Here's one example from Psalm 38:1 — "O Lord, do not rebuke me in your anger or discipline me in your wrath." In only three verses we see the emotions of love, regret, heartache, anger and wrath. So yes, God does have emotions. We have them because He has them. "So God created mankind in his own image, in the image of God he created them." (Genesis 1:27)

Genesis 6:6, which I quoted in the previous paragraph, is important for this discussion. It not only shows that God has emotions, it also shows that our actions can affect God's emotions. Look at verse 5: "The LORD saw how great the wickedness of the human race had become on the earth, and that every inclination of the thoughts of the human heart was only evil all the time." That's why "the LORD regretted that he had made human beings on the earth, and his heart was deeply troubled." This is only one example. There are many others.

That brings us back to the question — if you knew you could do something that would make God happy, would you do it?

A very natural response to that question would be, "What would make God happy?" Let's find out.

Two short parables in Luke 15, verses 4 through 10, talk about one thing that makes God very happy.

> "Suppose one of you has a hundred sheep and loses one of them. Doesn't he leave the ninety-nine in the open country and go after the lost sheep until he finds it? And when he finds it, he

joyfully puts it on his shoulders and goes home. Then he calls his friends and neighbors together and says, 'Rejoice with me; I have found my lost sheep.' I tell you that in the same way there will be more rejoicing in heaven over one sinner who repents than over ninety-nine righteous persons who do not need to repent.

"Or suppose a woman has ten silver coins and loses one. Doesn't she light a lamp, sweep the house and search carefully until she finds it? And when she finds it, she calls her friends and neighbors together and says, 'Rejoice with me; I have found my lost coin.' In the same way, I tell you, there is rejoicing in the presence of the angels of God over one sinner who repents."

You rejoice when you are happy and relieved, like when you finally find a credit card you thought you had lost. So all heaven rejoices when someone repents and accepts Jesus as their savior. Obviously that makes God happy, and that's where we have to start.

Okay, what else can make God happy? I could name some other things, but I'd only be scratching the surface. There's a big list of things we can do that will make God happy. A lot of it involves obedience, turning away from and rejecting things that make Him sad or angry. That's not easy for any of us, but God says it's necessary.

This question has changed the way I look at the Bible. Now when I read something that talks about my behavior, and the Bible says a lot about how we should behave, I ask myself, "Does this behavior make God happy, sad or angry?" Our actions have consequences for us and also for God.

And consider this — we saw earlier that we have emotions because God has them. So if we experience discouragement, then God must know it, too, at least in a theoretical sense. In other words, He may not experience discouragement the way we do, but He certainly knows what it is. We saw in Genesis 6 that God definitely gets disgusted and disappointed.

And if the coronavirus activity and rioting in the summer of 2020 have us down, how do you think God feels? He must be as disgusted as we are, maybe even more. Some people are thinking things can't get any worse and the End Times must be starting, but Jesus told us He won't return until the Father says the time is right. Nothing we can say or do will change that, but until then we need to be busy doing what we know we should do, especially when we don't want to. It won't be easy, but it will encourage the people around us and make God happy. And when we try to encourage others, someone will find a way to encourage you, too, like my young friend did for me two weeks ago. Let's get the encouragement going, so every one of us can be encouraged! And let's start now.

Call me Barnabas for the next few minutes, even though my name is Carl. Barnabas means "son of encouragement." That's who I want to be, a son of encouragement to you.

My friends know I'm weird. Some of them like it; many have come to accept it and the rest are... it's hard to know what other people think. I think the Apostle Paul would be okay with me, because people thought he was weird, too. Let's look at what he said to the Ephesians in chapter 5, verses 1 through 21:

> "Follow God's example, therefore, as dearly loved children and walk in the way of love, just as Christ loved us and gave himself up for us as a fragrant offering and sacrifice to God.

> "But among you there must not be even a hint of sexual immorality, or of any kind of impurity, or of greed, because these are improper for God's holy people. Nor should there be obscenity, foolish talk or coarse joking, which are out of place, but rather thanksgiving. For of this you can be sure: No immoral, impure or greedy person—such a person is an idolater—has any inheritance in the kingdom of Christ and of God. Let no one deceive you with empty words, for because of such things God's wrath comes on those who are disobedient. Therefore do not be partners with them.

> "For you were once darkness, but now you are light in the Lord. Live as children of light (for the fruit of the light consists in all goodness, righteousness and truth) and find out what pleases the Lord. Have nothing to do with the fruitless deeds of darkness, but rather expose them. It is shameful even to mention what the disobedient do in secret. But everything exposed by the light becomes visible—and everything that is illuminated becomes a light. This is why it is said: 'Wake up, sleeper, rise from the dead, and Christ will shine on you.'

> "Be very careful, then, how you live—not as unwise but as wise, making the most of every opportunity, because the days are evil. Therefore do not be foolish, but understand what the Lord's will is. Do not get drunk on wine, which leads to debauchery. Instead, be filled with the Spirit, speaking to one another with

psalms, hymns, and songs from the Spirit. Sing and make music from your heart to the Lord, always giving thanks to God the Father for everything, in the name of our Lord Jesus Christ.

"Submit to one another out of reverence for Christ."

People thought Paul was weird because of the way he lived his life. The way he put Jesus first in literally everything he did made him very different from the people around him.

It's okay to be weird. You could be into Japanese monster movies or Game of Thrones or motorcycles or genre fiction or whatever you're into, BUT we need to be careful about how we live. Paul's point is that we need to show the people around us that we are more into Jesus Christ than anything else. In verse 17 he said, "Do not be foolish, but understand what the Lord's will is." God's will is that we come out of the closet, so to speak, and openly obey Jesus Christ and His teaching. Paul talks about how we can do that in the passage we just read.

We can be weird and follow Jesus, but being weird for Jesus has to come first. Now there's an encouraging thought – we can be weird for Jesus, so let's be weird for Jesus!

Let's read Psalm 19:7-14 today.

> "The law of the Lord is perfect, refreshing the soul. The statutes of the Lord are trustworthy, making wise the simple. The precepts of the Lord are right, giving joy to the heart. The commands of the Lord are radiant, giving light to the eyes. The fear of the Lord is pure, enduring forever. The decrees of the Lord are firm, and all of them are righteous.
>
> "They are more precious than gold, than much pure gold; they are sweeter than honey, than honey from the honeycomb. By them your servant is warned; in keeping them there is great reward. But who can discern their own errors? Forgive my hidden faults. Keep your servant also from willful sins; may they not rule over me. Then I will be blameless, innocent of great transgression.
>
> "May these words of my mouth and this meditation of my heart be pleasing in your sight, Lord, my Rock and my Redeemer."

King David begins by telling us what God's Word can do for us. God's law is perfect and refreshes the soul. We can trust God's statutes; they make us wise. His precepts are right and give joy to our hearts. His decrees are firm and righteous.

In the Psalms and throughout the Old Testament the word law refers to God's instruction or teaching. The other terms David uses are more specific and the distinctions between them are not very clear in English. I quoted the NIV, and other translations will plug some of those same words into different verses. I do NOT know Hebrew; I can only tell you the English definitions of these words and admit there is some overlap in those definitions. A statute is a law given without any reason or justification. That sounds like what we now call a mandate. Precepts are guiding principles or rules that are used to control, influence or regulate conduct (the Ten Commandments are good examples of precepts). A command is something we are expected to obey. Some translations say judgments or ordinances instead of decrees, which are statements like "from now on, this is how it's going to be." Clear as mud? Let's move on, anyway.

Does your soul feel dried up and worn out? Do you want to be wise? Has your heart lost its joy? Has the light gone out of your eyes? Is that what's bothering you, my friend? If so, verses 7 & 8 of Psalm 19 tell you what can fix that. You need to learn and follow God's laws, statutes, precepts, commands and decrees.

God's Word is sweeter than the purest honey. That means it's the most pleasing and satisfying thing we can have. God's Word is also more precious than the purest gold. That means it's the best kind of wealth or treasure we can have. God's Word is also a warning to us and it says there is a reward for us when we obey.

David shows a lot of wisdom in verse 12 when he says, "But who can discern their own errors?" If you're like me (and weirdness has nothing to do with this), you can't see your own errors, either. Maybe we don't realize what we're doing is not what God told us to do. And maybe we let ourselves do some things when we're alone that we'd never do when other people are around. We need to pray as David did in verses 12 & 13: "Forgive my hidden faults. Keep your servant also from willful sins; may they not rule over me. Then I will be blameless, innocent of great transgression."

We too can be "innocent of great transgression." Does that mean our sinning days are over? No, not at all. Don't forget, in 2 Samuel 11 David had a man killed so he could take that man's wife for himself. David is also called a man after God's own heart. That means he learned the secret. He knew what to do to get right with God again. The first step is to acknowledge your sin, then repent of your sin, confess it to God and ask His forgiveness. After that we need to get back into the Bible, that sweet and precious treasure we read about a few minutes ago, soak it up the way a dry sponge soaks up water and obey what it tells us to do. That is not easy, but that's what it takes. We can be forgiven and get close to God again! If that's not encouraging, I don't know what is.

May these words of my mouth and this meditation of my heart be pleasing in your sight, Lord, my Rock and my Redeemer.

Here's my latest encouraging word, this time from Luke 8:22 – 25.

> "One day Jesus said to his disciples, 'Let us go over to the other side of the lake.' So they got into a boat and set out. As they sailed, he fell asleep. A squall came down on the lake, so that the boat was being swamped, and they were in great danger.
>
> "The disciples went and woke him, saying, "Master, Master, we're going to drown!' "

Let's stop there for a minute. A squall, according to Dictionary.com, is "any local storm on navigable water that is typically sudden and severe, with strong winds often accompanied by precipitation and sometimes thunder and lightning" and the disciples were caught in one. Verse 23 says their boat was getting swamped and they were in big trouble.

Can you remember a time when something suddenly came upon you and put you in serious trouble? I know I can. Or maybe you're facing some other kind of storm? Cry out to Jesus, as the disciples did, "Master, I'm going to drown!" If you haven't, you still can.

Let's go back to the historical account, starting in verse 24.

> "He [Jesus] got up and rebuked the wind and the raging waters; the storm subsided, and all was calm. 'Where is your faith?' he asked his disciples.
>
> "In fear and amazement they asked one another, 'Who is this? He commands even the winds and the water, and they obey him.' "

The verb rebuke means "to express sharp, stern disapproval; reprove; reprimand," again taken from Dictionary.com. That definition uses a few other words we don't often hear. When you reprove someone, you strongly disapprove of something they said or did. To reprimand means "to reprove or rebuke severely, especially in a formal way."

It's pretty clear Jesus did not approve of the storm. He spoke to it sharply and sternly, and it stopped. We don't know what he said, but it's easy to see why He said it from His next statement, "Where is your faith?" This storm took the disciple's faith past the breaking point. Some people think

Jesus chose to sleep to show the disciples how weak their faith was, but I don't agree. I think Jesus thought their faith should have been strong enough to handle their situation. I think He was more disappointed with the disciples' lack of faith than with the storm.

Here's my point. Jesus still delivered the disciples from the storm, even though they were weak and pretty much failed this test. Jesus may have hoped for a better reaction from them, but He still had their best interests in mind and saved them in a spectacular way. He can and will do the same for you, and that's encouraging!

The disciples had enough sense to call on Jesus for help. Have you asked Jesus to help you through your squall? Have you cried out to Jesus about the problems we face in this world? A number of potential solutions are floating around, but they won't be enough. Laws or politics don't change people; they only try to regulate us. (That's as political as I'm going to get.) People themselves need to change, to become more loving and respectful and forgiving, and only Jesus Christ can change people. Not only does He want to help you through your crisis, He wants to transform you "by the renewing of your mind. Then you will be able to test and approve what God's will is." (Romans 12:2) And that's encouraging, too.

WORD 36   The Parable of the Fantastic Father   8-16-20

Maybe you've seen this on Facebook. I've heard it was there, but I missed it. I read it in the May 2020 issue of the "Bridges for Peace" newsletter. The original post was from Israel and in Hebrew, and I'm told it was beautifully written, even poetic. The English translation clearly and eloquently speaks to what we've all been going through at this point in time. I wish I could credit the author, but I understand the original post was anonymous, so I cannot.

> "We have taken nature for granted; and now we are not allowed to leave the house.
>
> "We have disrespected our parents; and now we cannot see them in person.
>
> "We have treated our teachers with contempt; and now educational institutions are closed.
>
> "We have squandered our money on things we don't need; and now shopping malls have shut down.
>
> "We have more cars than we need; and now the roads are empty.
>
> "We have ceased to really connect with others; and now we are in isolation.
>
> "We have placed an importance on external beauty; and now our faces are covered with masks.
>
> "We can't keep on as if there is no tomorrow, because if we do, tomorrow will not come.
>
> "We all need to pause and take account of our lives, because the gift of this virus is we have received a second chance."

God has blessed us. In fact, God has GREATLY blessed us. And God is still blessing us. As people so often do, we have not only ignored those blessings, we have even thrown them away. In Luke 15:11-32 Jesus talked about a guy who did exactly that...

"There was a man who had two sons. The younger one said to his father, 'Father, give me my share of the estate.' So he divided his property between them.

"Not long after that, the younger son got together all he had, set off for a distant country and there squandered his wealth in wild living. After he had spent everything, there was a severe famine in that whole country, and he began to be in need. So he went and hired himself out to a citizen of that country, who sent him to his fields to feed pigs. He longed to fill his stomach with the pods that the pigs were eating, but no one gave him anything.

"When he came to his senses, he said, 'How many of my father's hired servants have food to spare, and here I am starving to death! I will set out and go back to my father and say to him: Father, I have sinned against heaven and against you. I am no longer worthy to be called your son; make me like one of your hired servants.' So he got up and went to his father.

"But while he was still a long way off, his father saw him and was filled with compassion for him; he ran to his son, threw his arms around him and kissed him.

"The son said to him, 'Father, I have sinned against heaven and against you. I am no longer worthy to be called your son.'

"But the father said to his servants, 'Quick! Bring the best robe and put it on him. Put a ring on his finger and sandals on his feet. Bring the fattened calf and kill it. Let's have a feast and celebrate. For this son of mine was dead and is alive again; he was lost and is found.' So they began to celebrate.

"Meanwhile, the older son was in the field. When he came near the house, he heard music and dancing. So he called one of the servants and asked him what was going on. 'Your brother has come,' he replied, 'and your father has killed the fattened calf because he has him back safe and sound.'

"The older brother became angry and refused to go in. So his father went out and pleaded with him. But he answered his father, 'Look! All these years I've been slaving for you and never disobeyed your orders. Yet you never gave me even a young goat so I could celebrate with my friends. But when this son of yours who has squandered your property with prostitutes comes home, you kill the fattened calf for him!'

"'My son,' the father said, 'you are always with me, and everything I have is yours. But we had to celebrate and be glad, because this brother of yours was dead and is alive again; he was lost and is found.'"

Many people call this the Parable of the Prodigal Son. The word prodigal, according to Dictionary.com, means wastefully or recklessly extravagant. Calling this parable the Prodigal Son, however, places our emphasis or focus on the son. Should we be like the son? While there are lessons we can learn from the son, we learn more about his Dad. We learn how we should treat people who regret and repent of the way they have treated us. We learn forgiveness, love, respect and acceptance; we need to know and practice all of those characteristics. Ever since I realized this I've called this passage the Parable of the Fantastic Father.

After the son realized he had wasted and lost everything his father had given him, he repented. He realized and admitted his errors, regretted his actions, was sorry and decided to turn his life around and apologize. His father forgave him and welcomed him back into the family. His older brother reacted out of pride and ego, basically saying, "Hey, Dad, what about me?" We know what their father told him. "My son, you are always with me, and everything I have is yours. But we had to celebrate and be glad, because this brother of yours was dead and is alive again; he was lost and is found."

In Luke 15:10 Jesus gave us the main point of this story before He told it. "There is rejoicing in the presence of the angels of God over one sinner who repents." My point is that this parable also applies to us. Don't forget, when the story began the son was together with his father. For some unknown reason the son decided to leave. When he returned a changed man, however, his father welcomed him back. We turn away from God, too, more often than we care to admit. If we repent of our wicked ways, God will not only forgive us, He will also take us back again.

God wants us with Him and He wants to bless us. That's encouraging. When we make bad decisions and leave Him, He wants us to repent and come back. When we do, He celebrates and throws a party! That's encouraging, too. We, however, need to stay close to God, and that's a challenge.

WORD 37   The Vine & the Branches   8-23-2020

Hey homeowners, do you have a vine in your yard? We do. It spread to several places, but we took out some of it, because it was interfering with other plants in my wife's gardens. One section of vine that we left alone has completely overgrown a wire fence by the street. A couple summers ago a neighbor who is a serious gardener asked if he could pick the berries. About a week later he surprised us with a jar of jam! We had no idea those little berries would be worth eating, but we were happy to be proved wrong.

Jesus once talked about a vine. Let's read what He said in John 15:1-11.

> "I am the true vine, and my Father is the gardener. He cuts off every branch in me that bears no fruit, while every branch that does bear fruit he prunes so that it will be even more fruitful. You are already clean because of the word I have spoken to you. Remain in me, as I also remain in you. No branch can bear fruit by itself; it must remain in the vine. Neither can you bear fruit unless you remain in me.

> "I am the vine; you are the branches. If you remain in me and I in you, you will bear much fruit; apart from me you can do nothing. If you do not remain in me, you are like a branch that is thrown away and withers; such branches are picked up, thrown into the fire and burned. If you remain in me and my words remain in you, ask whatever you wish, and it will be done for you. This is to my Father's glory, that you bear much fruit, showing yourselves to be my disciples.

> "As the Father has loved me, so have I loved you. Now remain in my love. If you keep my commands, you will remain in my love, just as I have kept my Father's commands and remain in his love. I have told you this so that my joy may be in you and that your joy may be complete."

Why would someone keep a vine? My wife and I kept one because it made a nice divider between our yard and the street. To our neighbor, though, the berries could be a source of food. He made them into jam. If you have enough berries, maybe you could make wine. So the purpose of the vine is to produce useful berries or fruit.

Jesus started by saying, "I am the true vine, and my Father is the gardener." The gardener, of course, takes care of the vine. In verse 5 Jesus said, "I am the vine; you are the branches." He is talking to His disciples, the people who are following Him and trying to learn from Him. That should include us.

Obviously we are supposed to produce good fruit, and the more the better. As verses 5 and 8 put it, "If you remain in me and I in you, you will bear much fruit... This is to my Father's glory, that you bear much fruit." The only way we can bear fruit, according to verse 5, is "if you remain in me and I in you... apart from me you can do nothing." Jesus is talking about a decision we face, to remain in Him or not to remain in Him. As with any decision, there are consequences, which are explained in verses 6 & 7: "If you do not remain in me, you are like a branch that is thrown away and withers; such branches are picked up, thrown into the fire and burned. If you remain in me and my words remain in you, ask whatever you wish, and it will be done for you."

Don't forget, fruit is a sign that the branch is alive. A branch without fruit is not healthy and could be dying. We didn't pay enough attention to our vine. We didn't see a dead branch until it was obviously dead. When we found one, though, we did the same thing the Master Gardener did – burn it in our fire pit.

But what does it mean, to remain in Jesus? That's what the closing verses of John 15 talk about. First, verse 9 says the Father's love comes to us through Jesus. Then we remain in His love by keeping His commands (verse 10). When we do that, we will have His joy, which will complete our joy (verse 11).

Jesus' point is in verses 4 and 5: "No branch can bear fruit by itself; it must remain in the vine. Neither can you bear fruit unless you remain in me... apart from me you can do nothing."

But what kind of fruit does God like? God likes several kinds of fruit, just as we do. After all, we are made in His image. Maybe combining verses 5 and 11 will help. If we remain in or stay close to Jesus and obey Him by keeping His commands, we will produce much good fruit. In a nutshell (if you'll pardon the expression), anything we can do that makes God happy is a fruit He likes. And that's encouraging!

My wife and I were happy to learn that the berries on our vine made a good jam. Let's all make God happy by producing good fruit.

By the end of the summer in even numbered years all citizens of the US of A must realize that we have an election coming up. A flood of political advertising is on the TV, in our mailboxes, on the radio, even making our phones ring. We also know that more is coming. Both the Democratic and Republican parties have held their national conventions and endorsed their candidates. Now they are trying to convince us to vote for one of them.

Over the past few weeks I've heard a number of people say they don't like any of the presidential candidates this year. Many of these people aren't so much wondering, "Who should I vote for?" as they are asking, "Why should I vote this year?" I understand those doubts. I've faced them myself.

I cannot and will not tell you who to vote for. That would be patronizing and insulting. I can and will, however, tell you why to vote, based on what the Bible teaches. That should be encouraging, which is what I want to do.

Someone just thought or said, "Wait a minute. I've been reading the Bible for years and it doesn't say a thing about voting." If you mean the word "vote" is not in the Bible, I have to admit you're right. The Bible does talk about a Christian's civic responsibilities, however, and I think we'll see some principles in those passages that will apply to voting.

We have to start by realizing we have dual citizenship. I expect the majority of my readers are US citizens, but that doesn't matter — we are all citizens of some country. We are also children and heirs of God (Galatians 3:26-29) and therefore citizens of God's kingdom (Philippians 3:20). Should one citizenship be more important to us than the other? The Bible is clear on that – NOTHING should be more important to us than our relationship with God. So our heavenly citizenship takes precedence over our earthly citizenship.

All the same, God expects us to be good citizens of our countries. We have certain responsibilities, which we need to take seriously yet reconcile with the Bible. Jesus Himself acknowledged this when He said, "'Love the Lord your God with all your heart and with all your soul and with all your mind.' This is the first and greatest commandment. And the second is like it: 'Love your neighbor as yourself.' All the Law and the Prophets hang on these two commandments." (Matthew 22:37-40) Loving your neighbor as yourself includes being a good citizen. Let's also read I Peter 2:13-17.

> "Submit yourselves for the Lord's sake to every human authority: whether to the emperor, as the supreme authority, or to governors, who are sent by him to punish those who do wrong and to commend those who do right. For it is God's will that by doing good you should silence the ignorant talk of foolish people. Live as free people, but do not use your freedom as a cover-up for evil; live as God's slaves. Show proper respect to everyone, love the family of believers, fear God, honor the emperor."

In order to understand what Peter is saying, we need to know what system of government was in place for his audience. During Jesus' earthly years Israel was a part of the Roman Empire. Pontius Pilate, the regional governor for Israel, was responsible to Tiberius Caesar Augustus, the Roman emperor, but those leaders changed several times during the first century. That's why Peter refers to an emperor and governors.

Someone is probably thinking that we cannot make an adequate comparison between our constitutional republic and the dictatorial empire of Peter's time. You're missing my point. We're not talking about the system of government; we're talking about how we Christians as citizens should respond to it.

And how does Peter say Christians should respond to their government? The answer is in verses 15 through 17: "By doing good you should silence the ignorant talk of foolish people. Live as free people, but do not use your freedom as a cover-up for evil; live as God's slaves. Show proper respect to everyone, love the family of believers, fear God, honor the emperor." This obedient and respectful lifestyle is one way we can love our neighbors and our country.

Our government expects us to vote. And I think we agree that voting is a good thing. Peter told us to submit to and obey our government, so there is one Biblical reason to vote.

Now let's look at Romans 13:1-7

"Let everyone be subject to the governing authorities, for there is no authority except that which God has established. The authorities that exist have been established by God. Consequently, whoever rebels against the authority is rebelling against what God has instituted, and those who do so will bring judgment on themselves. For rulers hold no terror for those who do right, but for those who do wrong. Do you want to be free from fear of the one in authority? Then do what is right and you will be commended. For the one in authority is God's servant for your good. But if you do wrong, be afraid, for rulers do not bear the sword for no reason. They are God's servants, agents of wrath to bring punishment on the wrongdoer. Therefore, it is necessary to submit to the authorities, not only because of possible punishment but also as a matter of conscience.

"This is also why you pay taxes, for the authorities are God's servants, who give their full time to governing. Give to everyone what you owe them: If you owe taxes, pay taxes; if revenue, then revenue; if respect, then respect; if honor, then honor."

This passage tells us several things. One, that God established the concept of government. Two, rebelling against the government is also rebelling against God. Three, the government serves God in one way or another. Four, we should submit to the government "not only because of possible punishment but also as a matter of conscience." And five, give the government whatever you may owe it.

Paul's conclusion echoes Jesus' words in Matthew 22:21: "So give back to Caesar what is Caesar's, and to God what is God's." We live in both kingdoms and have to satisfy both of them. We should obey and cooperate with our earthly government until that obedience or cooperation conflicts with what God expects of us, because God's kingdom has priority.

Our government expects us to vote. In Romans 13:7 Paul told us, "Give to everyone what you owe them." To paraphrase Matthew 22:21, "Give back to the government what belongs to the government." That is another Biblical reason to vote.

In Romans 13:2 Paul said, "Whoever rebels against the authority is

Going Viral – Encouraging Words for Discouraging Times

rebelling against what God has instituted, and those who do so will bring judgment on themselves." A third Biblical reason to vote is to avoid God's judgment.

Romans 13:5 says, "It is necessary to submit to the authorities, not only because of possible punishment but also as a matter of conscience." The government would not punish you for not voting, but would your conscience bother you? According to this verse, that's also a good reason to vote.

It's true that voting is not legally required of us. A person could choose not to vote and there are no immediate personal consequences. But consider this – how does choosing not to vote show the people around you that you love and respect them? How does choosing not to vote show that you are a responsible citizen? If you choose not to vote, what's to stop you from refusing to obey the government in some other way? And if you start to rebel against the government, where will it stop? What would keep you from eventually rebelling against God?

I know this subject can be controversial. That's not a bad thing; controversy forces us to think. Does it make you uncomfortable? Perhaps you should reexamine your priorities. Maybe you are making your earthly citizenship more important than your heavenly citizenship.

I've stated my position. I see no reason to debate it, because to me the Bible is clear about it. If you think I'm wrong, prove it from the Bible. And say it to me personally.

Knowing why we should vote is encouraging. Now some of you are wondering, "How do I choose who to vote for?" That's a completely different subject. Let's talk about it next week.

By this time of year during even numbered years all US citizens must realize that we have an election coming up. We are inundated by political advertising on the TV, in our mailboxes and on the radio. It even makes our phones ring and more is coming. Both the Democratic and Republican parties endorsed their candidates at their national conventions. Now they want to convince us to vote for one of them. Oh, boy...

Recently I've heard a number of people say they don't like any of the presidential candidates. How should we choose who we should vote for when we don't like any of the candidates? I'm glad you asked!

Last week, you remember, we saw that we believers have dual citizenship and that being a good Christian includes being a good citizen of our countries. Since God established our human authorities (see Romans 13:1 and John 19:11), it makes sense to choose leaders who follow Christian principles. But how can we determine that?

We need to start with their political affiliation. I am a US citizen, so I'll use the USA as an example. There are two major political parties in this country, the Republican Party and the Democratic Party, along with several smaller ones. These parties have their own ideologies or platforms, which their endorsed candidates share. These ideologies are what make each political party unique.

Dictionary.com says the word ideology means "a system of ideas and ideals, especially one which forms the basis of economic or political theory and policy." In other words, it's a broad or general description of that political party's concept of governing the country.

A political party may not have a position on a specific issue, however. The candidates themselves will have their own positions on those issues. This is what can make two candidates from the same party different.

Thanks to the Internet, we can easily look up these platforms and positions. Then we can compare them to what the Bible teaches us to see which candidate is closer to God's standards. We as responsible citizens need to do this research in order to choose the best available candidate.

But how can a book as old as the Bible speak to today's issues? The truth is, most of our issues have been around for a long time. For example, these days we're hearing people say black lives matter. The Bible talks about loving our neighbor (see Leviticus 19:18 and Matthew 5:43) and valuing human life (John 3:16). The Bible also says a lot about justice and human rights. In fact, the Bible is the best guidebook available about how to help people get along together.

So reading the Bible will help you choose who to vote for? The short answer is yes. The better you know the Bible, the better you'll be able to choose the best available candidate. And, of course, we should pray about deciding which candidate to vote for. God can and will give you wisdom, according to James 1:5.

So, in conclusion, choosing who to vote for is not about personalities or idiosyncrasies or how they make us feel. It's about policies and issues and Biblical truth. It's about finding the candidate who best represents what we as Christians think is important, whether that person is a believer or not. That's going to take time and effort, but it's a part of our responsibility as Christians and citizens. So start doing this homework now, while you still have some time.

WORD 40   The End is Near   9-20-2020

My friends, the time has come to end these messages.

I chose to use whatever ability I have as a writer and teacher to encourage those who needed it, but never intended to continue indefinitely. I had a window of opportunity and opened it. I thought this coronovirus situation would be pretty much over by the middle of the summer of 2020. Maybe I should have believed the people who said it would continue this long. Then again, those people also made other claims that were not as accurate…

The honest truth is my family needs me back. Yes, I have a responsibility to you guys; I am my brothers (and sisters) keeper. I also have a greater responsibility to my wife and family. They have been missing me and not getting my best when I can be with them.

So that is that, as they say. (Whoever they are.) Someone suggested I collect these writings into book form. I like that idea, and want to make that happen.

I will leave you with one final word of encouragement, however, from Psalm 147.

> Praise the LORD.
>
> How good it is to sing praises to our God, how pleasant and fitting to praise him!
>
> The LORD builds up Jerusalem; he gathers the exiles of Israel. He heals the brokenhearted and binds up their wounds. He determines the number of the stars and calls them each by name. Great is our Lord and mighty in power; his understanding has no limit. The LORD sustains the humble but casts the wicked to the ground.
>
> Sing to the LORD with grateful praise; make music to our God on the harp.
>
> He covers the sky with clouds; he supplies the earth with rain and makes grass grow on the hills. He provides food for the cattle and for the young ravens when they call.

His pleasure is not in the strength of the horse, nor his delight in the legs of the warrior; the LORD delights in those who fear him, who put their hope in his unfailing love.

Extol the LORD, Jerusalem; praise your God, Zion.

He strengthens the bars of your gates and blesses your people within you. He grants peace to your borders and satisfies you with the finest of wheat.

He sends his command to the earth; his word runs swiftly. He spreads the snow like wool and scatters the frost like ashes. He hurls down his hail like pebbles. Who can withstand his icy blast? He sends his word and melts them; he stirs up his breezes, and the waters flow.

He has revealed his word to Jacob, his laws and decrees to Israel. He has done this for no other nation; they do not know his laws.

Praise the LORD.

Okay, this one will be my last word.

We've seen some craziness in this first week of November 2020, some of the craziest craziness of a crazy year. Half of the country is saying "all hope is gone" and the other half is saying "our hope is restored." That probably means about half the country needs antidepressants and the other half needs the opposite, whatever that's called. I'm going out on a limb here and saying Kanye West will not be president of the USA in 2021. Call it a gut feeling...

The honest truth is that these so-called election results don't change anything important. A friend of mine found a list on Facebook of ten vitally important things the election will NOT change. Maybe you've already seen them, but they are worth reading again. Here they are, with my own addition at number 11.

1) God will still be on His throne.

2) Jesus will still be King of kings and Lord of lords.

3) The Bible will still have the answer to every problem.

4) The tomb will still be empty.

5) Jesus will still be the only way to Heaven.

6) Prayer will still work – it will still make a difference and God will still answer prayer.

7) The cross, not the government, will still be our salvation.

8) There will still be room at the cross.

9) Jesus will still save anyone who places their faith and trust in Him.

10) God will still be with us always – He will never leave us or forsake us.

11) Jesus is still coming back!

Once again I leave you (I think), and this time with Psalm 34.

"I will extol the Lord at all times; his praise will always be on my lips. I will glory in the Lord; let the afflicted hear and rejoice. Glorify the Lord with me; let us exalt his name together.

"I sought the Lord, and he answered me; he delivered me from all my fears. Those who look to him are radiant; their faces are never covered with shame. This poor man called, and the Lord heard him; he saved him out of all his troubles. The angel of the Lord encamps around those who fear him, and he delivers them.

"Taste and see that the Lord is good; blessed is the one who takes refuge in him. Fear the Lord, you his holy people, for those who fear him lack nothing. The lions may grow weak and hungry, but those who seek the Lord lack no good thing. Come, my children, listen to me; I will teach you the fear of the Lord. Whoever of you loves life and desires to see many good days, keep your tongue from evil and your lips from telling lies. Turn from evil and do good; seek peace and pursue it.

"The eyes of the Lord are on the righteous, and his ears are attentive to their cry; but the face of the Lord is against those who do evil, to blot out their name from the earth.

"The righteous cry out, and the Lord hears them; he delivers them from all their troubles. The Lord is close to the brokenhearted and saves those who are crushed in spirit.

"The righteous person may have many troubles, but the Lord delivers him from them all; he protects all his bones, not one of them will be broken.

"Evil will slay the wicked; the foes of the righteous will be condemned. The Lord will rescue his servants; no one who takes refuge in him will be condemned."

David wrote this psalm at a time when the nation of Israel was so divided; it was practically two separate nations. Let's join with him and extol the Lord at ALL times (especially now) and ALWAYS have his praise on our lips. Call out to God and He will not only hear you, but will also answer you, deliver you from all your fears and save you from all your troubles. He will provide many good things for us IF we seek Him, take refuge in Him, turn from evil to do good and seek and pursue peace. God WILL rescue His servants, so let's serve Him, starting today.

I'm claiming Proverbs 22:18 right now – "There is surely a future hope for you, and your hope will not be cut off."

Don't forget, in this nation of elephants and donkeys, God is calling us to be His sheep. (I wish I could take credit for that great line, but I can't. I borrowed it from my pastor, who can't remember where he heard it.) So, my fellow sheep, let me encourage you to be the best sheep you can be!

WORD 42   A Call to Arms!   12-6-2020

Nearly a year ago we first heard reports of a highly contagious disease in China. Less than three months later it had spread around the world and far enough into the USA to cause a massive disruption here. Now, when we are told a vaccine is almost ready, that virus is surging again.

During a national crisis a president will often call for a day of prayer. Why are we waiting for the government to ask us to pray?

A number of people are not happy with the results of the November election. (My biggest concern, however, is election integrity.) The election itself may be over, but the process of choosing the next president of the USA is not. I expect all US citizens know our next president is not chosen by the popular vote. It's up to the Electoral College, which has deadlines. I found a blog on bipartisanpolicy.org that explains it. Here is their summary.

> "The three critical milestones taking place this December are (1) the Safe Harbor deadline, (2) the casting of electors' votes, and (3) the deadline for receipt of these results by the President of the Senate.

> "(1) U.S. Code requires that states resolve all election-related disputes six days before electors cast their votes. States are expected to complete recounts, resolve any legal challenges, and certify results by this date, commonly known as the "Safe Harbor" deadline... they must deliver the certificates to the U.S. Archivist and the state's slate of electors no later than December 14...

> "(2) U.S. Code dictates that electors shall meet and vote on the Monday after the second Wednesday in December of presidential election years. This year, that date falls on December 14...

> "(3) The aforementioned certificates—each including the names of electors, the electors' votes, and the state's certified election results—must be delivered to all relevant parties by the fourth Wednesday in December, or December 23 in 2020... After certificates are delivered on December 23, the electors' job is complete."

I think most US citizens now realize there were "election-related disputes" in the 2020 election. Individual states have to resolve election related issues 6 days before that state's slate of electors meet and vote on Monday December 14, 2020. 14 – 6 = 8, so each state has until Tuesday December 8 to resolve all election-related disputes, whatever they might be. And today is Sunday December 6.

This means there is still time, because the process is not over. Members of the Electoral College are expected to follow the results of the popular vote in their state, but not every state requires it. If you are not satisfied with the current standing of the popular vote, and from what I've heard many people are not satisfied with what they have heard, PRAY. Prayer does and will make a difference.

We know God will not answer selfish prayers, so we need to pray for what He wants, not what we want. I recommend that we pray NOW for these things —

1) that the truth of our election would be revealed,

2) that our system would be fixed,

3) that the vaccine would be effective (95% effective means 1 out of every 20 people will have some kind of problem), and

4) that God's will is done.

Time is running out, so spread the word! The Electoral College has overturned the popular vote before. All believers need to pray for the entire process of this and every election.

WORD 43   The Last Word   12-31-2020

As I sit to write this, I'm in the last hours of 2020. That must make this the last word...

A lot of people are feeling drained of life these days, dried up and dead. The prophet Ezekiel once wrote about a situation like that. This is what he said.

> "The hand of the Lord was on me, and he brought me out by the Spirit of the Lord and set me in the middle of a valley; it was full of bones. He led me back and forth among them, and I saw a great many bones on the floor of the valley, bones that were very dry. He asked me, 'Son of man, can these bones live?'

> "I said, 'Sovereign Lord, you alone know.'

> "Then he said to me, 'Prophesy to these bones and say to them, "Dry bones, hear the word of the Lord! This is what the Sovereign Lord says to these bones: I will make breath enter you, and you will come to life. I will attach tendons to you and make flesh come upon you and cover you with skin; I will put breath in you, and you will come to life. Then you will know that I am the Lord."'

> "So I prophesied as I was commanded. And as I was prophesying, there was a noise, a rattling sound, and the bones came together, bone to bone. I looked, and tendons and flesh appeared on them and skin covered them, but there was no breath in them.

> "Then he said to me, 'Prophesy to the breath; prophesy, son of man, and say to it, "This is what the Sovereign Lord says: Come, breath, from the four winds and breathe into these slain, that they may live."' So I prophesied as he commanded me, and breath entered them; they came to life and stood up on their feet—a vast army.

> "Then he said to me: 'Son of man, these bones... say, "Our bones are dried up and our hope is gone; we are cut off." Therefore prophesy and say to them: "This is what the Sovereign Lord says: My people, I am going to open your graves and bring you up from them; I will bring you back... Then you, my people, will

know that I am the Lord, when I open your graves and bring you up from them. I will put my Spirit in you and you will live... Then you will know that I the Lord have spoken, and I have done it, declares the Lord."'" (Ezekiel 37:1-14)

Did you catch it? God is talking about His people! They felt dried up in their bones. They thought their hope was gone. They said they were cut off from God. Does that sound familiar? Does it describe you or maybe someone you know? So much of the church in America is like those dry and lifeless bones. God can raise and reassemble them quicker and more easily that we can put together Ikea furniture. Then He will put His Spirit in those rebuilt bodies and they will live!

Then again, maybe that's not you. Maybe you are saying, "2020 hasn't completely broken me. I'm not dead; I just don't have much life in me right now. My battery is low; I need a recharge." The apostle Paul talked about that in 2 Corinthians. See for yourself.

"We have this treasure in jars of clay to show that this all-surpassing power is from God and not from us. We are hard pressed on every side, but not crushed; perplexed, but not in despair; persecuted, but not abandoned; struck down, but not destroyed. We always carry around in our body the death of Jesus, so that the life of Jesus may also be revealed in our body. For we who are alive are always being given over to death for Jesus' sake, so that his life may also be revealed in our mortal body. So then, death is at work in us, but life is at work in you.

"It is written: 'I believed; therefore I have spoken.' Since we have that same spirit of faith, we also believe and therefore speak, because we know that the one who raised the Lord Jesus from the dead will also raise us with Jesus and present us with you to himself. All this is for your benefit, so that the grace that is reaching more and more people may cause thanksgiving to overflow to the glory of God.

"Therefore we do not lose heart. Though outwardly we are wasting away, yet inwardly we are being renewed day by day. For our light and momentary troubles are achieving for us an eternal glory that far outweighs them all. So we fix our eyes not on what is seen, but on what is unseen, since what is seen is temporary, but what is unseen is eternal." (2 Corinthians 4:7-18)

Those "jars of clay" in verse 7 are our human bodies. God enables us to endure so He can "show that this all-surpassing power is from God and not from us." Hard pressed on every side, but not crushed; perplexed, but not in despair; persecuted, but not abandoned; struck down, but not destroyed — maybe that was you in 2020. Okay, then, "do not lose heart. Though outwardly we are wasting away, yet inwardly we are being renewed day by day. For our light and momentary troubles are achieving for us an eternal glory that far outweighs them all. So we fix our eyes not on what is seen, but on what is unseen, since what is seen is temporary, but what is unseen is eternal." (v16-18)

According to those last few verses, 2020 is a "light and momentary trouble," meaning it is only temporary. (God said that, not me.) We might be wasting away on the outside, yet "inwardly we are being renewed day by day," which will bring us to an unseen and "eternal glory that far outweighs them all." That sounds pretty good, doesn't it?

But how can we be daily renewed during such a devastating experience as 2020 has been to so many people? Has God given us something, or maybe told us to do something, that can overpower this despair and bring healing to us and our country?

You might have noticed there are some strong hints about answers to those questions in the passages we have read today. Another one comes to my mind, though. While we cannot reduce God to a formula, He sometimes gives us a formula. We call them His promises. The one I'm thinking of starts off like this — "If My people who are called by My name will humble themselves and pray..." Yes, it's 2 Chronicles 7:14. We have looked at it before. It's the promise that began all my writings back in March. Maybe you should read it again and put it back into practice. It's the promise that will change our world and our lives. It will work because God said it will work.

What do we have to lose? Just look at what we could gain! Why not give it a chance? All we have to do is obey. And that's encouraging.

WORD 44   Never Too Late   **1-21-2021**

Yes, I'm at it again, one more time.

"It ain't over 'till it's over." A famous baseball player turned manager once said that, and he's right. It is NOT over. Don't let anyone tell you it's over. It's not over until the fat lady sings, which is not the best way to put it, but is a bit more accurate.

What am I babbling about? I think you know, but I'll tell you anyway.

Early in December I sent out a note about the timing involved with the election results. I think I may have misled some people and given a false impression. I never meant to say God must act on or before a certain date. If that's what you thought, I'm sorry about that and need to correct it.

What? Did I send out bad information? Not really, it was accurate, as far as it went. It was from an official source, which means it was made by people – frail and limited human beings. God doesn't recognize our deadlines or calendar; He is NOT limited by time. I know that and should have known better.

"You're babbling again, buddy. Start making sense, will you?" Okay, people, pay attention.

The best example I have comes from John 11. I think you're familiar with it, so I'll summarize.

Mary and Martha were sisters and very good friends of Jesus. They sent word to Him that their brother was seriously ill and urged Him to come quickly, but He couldn't or didn't. When Jesus finally arrived, Lazarus had already been dead for four days. Jesus went to the tomb and told them to roll away the stone. Martha reminded Him that it had been four days; there would be a bad odor (a dead body begins to decay after three days). Jesus asked them to believe and raised Lazarus from the dead.

There is another familiar story in Luke 8. Again, I will summarize.

A man named Jairus, a leader in the local synagogue, begged Jesus to come to his house and heal his only daughter, who was dying. They were not able to leave immediately; something important came up. When they were able to go, a messenger from Jairus' house arrived to say his daughter was dead and there was no point in bothering Jesus anymore. Jesus said to Jairus, "Don't be afraid; just believe, and she will be healed." When they arrived at the house Jesus raised the girl from the dead.

Jesus didn't follow human timetables in either account. He came at His time. Jesus didn't care about our science, what we think we know about the way things work, because He helped to create the universe, including our bodies, in the first place; He can make anything do what He wants it to do. When things looked WAY too late to these people, normal human beings like you and me, Jesus acted and performed a miracle.

I think you see my point. It is NEVER too late for God to act. If we believe He can do something, He CAN do it! I'll say this in words of one syllable, because that's the way I learned it – put your faith in God!

In Mark 9 Jesus healed a boy possessed by a spirit that wouldn't let him speak. The disciples couldn't help the boy. When Jesus arrived, the boy's father said to him, "If you can do anything, take pity on us and help us" (verse 22). Jesus replied, "'If you can'? Everything is possible for one who believes" (verse 23). Immediately the boy's father exclaimed, "I do believe; help me overcome my unbelief!" (verse 24) That's when the boy was delivered from the spirit that possessed him.

The New Testament was written in Greek. The people who translated it into English had a small problem, because the English language doesn't have a verb form of the word "faith." The closest we can come is to say "have faith." The Greek noun for faith, however, does has a verb form. It was translated "believe." To believe is to have faith.

But have faith in what? Faith must have an object; we need to have faith in something or someone. What should we believe in, or have faith in? It needs to be something strong or powerful enough to do what we hope it can do. In Mark 11:22 Jesus told us to "have faith in God."

"Help me overcome my unbelief." That sounds like something I would and should say more often. Time and again I want to believe something but am not sure I can believe it. Do you ever feel that way? Jesus answered that father's prayer. Why would He not answer when we ask the same thing?

Back when I attended public school I was taught several ways to recognize solid research and evidence, and not to simply accept someone's word when something seems ridiculous and should be ignored. Later, when my parents began to attend a church that believed God means what He says in the Bible and I finally understood what Jesus wanted to do in and for me, I learned that what I was taught in public school may be a good way to deal with the secular world, but I couldn't deal with God that way. God expects us to believe Him. Jesus said, "I am the way and the truth and the life." (John 14:6) Life with God is based on faith in God. I had to and came to accept God's word as right and true by faith. We all do.

There are still legitimate and unanswered procedural questions about this election. It's not over until those issues are resolved. It's not too late for God to work, either. So put your faith in God and keep on keeping on. God IS going to do something wonderful in this country, just wait and see! And that's encouraging.

Here it is, more than two years after the first case of COVID-19 was detected in the USA. Two long, disappointing frustrating and out of control years. The George Floyd riots were only a half hour drive from home and spread to the northwest instead of straight west, my direction. We've seen the mask mandates extended, with no end in sight. We've learned that these vaccines do NOT immunize us from the disease; we can take the vaccine and still get COVID-19. And we've been told we need booster shots for the vaccines. This state of emergency has gone on for so long; we're not convinced it will end. The 2020 election results and the incident, or whatever you want to call it, on January 6, 2021, affected all of us. I could go on, but I won't. (You're welcome.) We've seen so many things go against us that we're worn out, exhausted, discouraged. I think I've been through everything you have, except I didn't catch COVID yet, praise God. *[Author's note – that happened in February 2022.]*

Here's a good question – have we learned anything from all this? Maybe a better question is, what have I learned from all this?

I've realized that we cannot put our hope, faith or trust in any things or people on this planet. Does that mean we have no hope? No, I think that means we should put our hope, faith and trust into someone or something that's NOT on this planet!

No, I'm not going science fiction on you. I suppose I could, since I'm a big fan of science fiction, but it wouldn't help you. I'm going Jesus on you, because He can and will help you. I'll tell you the three most important things I've learned in the past two years. Maybe it will help you in some way.

First, I have learned again that not only is God still in control of the world, He will stay in control of the world. I'm reminded of something I would say at work — a day doesn't have to go the way I think it should in order to be a good day. I've often told people, "Today is a good day to have a good day." Those sayings may sound trite or cliché, but you can find those thoughts in the Bible.

In Deuteronomy 7:9 we read this, "Know therefore that the Lord your God is God; he is the faithful God, keeping his covenant of love to a thousand generations of those who love him and keep his commandments."

Psalm 42:5 says, "Why, my soul, are you downcast? Why so disturbed within me? Put your hope in God, for I will yet praise him, my Savior and my God."

And there's Psalm 56:4, which says, "In God, whose word I praise— in God I trust and am not afraid. What can mere mortals do to me?"

There's also Proverbs 3:5-6 — "Trust in the Lord with all your heart and lean not on your own understanding; in all your ways submit to him, and he will make your paths straight."

Jesus said something like that in the John 6:31-33 —

> "So do not worry, saying, 'What shall we eat?' or 'What shall we drink?' or 'What shall we wear?' For the pagans run after all these things, and your heavenly Father knows that you need them. But seek first his kingdom and his righteousness, and all these things will be given to you as well. Therefore do not worry about tomorrow, for tomorrow will worry about itself. Each day has enough trouble of its own."

In 1 Corinthians 1:9 we read, "God is faithful, who has called you into fellowship with his Son, Jesus Christ our Lord."

And that's just a start. There are LOTS of places in the Bible that tell us not only that God can be trusted during difficult times, but He is also in control of what happens to us and around us.

A second thing I have realized more fully is that this world is temporary. Through Jesus Christ I have eternal life (John 3:16). One of my favorite old gospel songs says, "This world is not my home; I'm just passing through." That means this world and all its troubles will end, but I won't. One day I will die or Jesus will return and everything will change for me. Paul talks about this in 2 Corinthians 5:1-10. When that happens, I will literally be in a better place. I will see my Lord and Savior face to face and I want to hear him say, "You did well, my friend."

The third thing I have realized could be the most important one. Now I better understand that I have things to do while I wait for my meeting with Jesus. Most people know that Jesus spoke about the end times in Matthew 24 and stop at the end of that chapter, but Jesus didn't stop there. In Matthew 25 He told us to be alert, to prepare and be ready for His return.

Consider this. In Acts 1, after Jesus rose into the clouds, did the 12 disciples sit on the side of the mountain and wait for Him to return? No, they did not. Why not? Because Jesus gave them an assignment (see Matthew 28:19-20) and told them to get busy. I have my assignment, too, and I think this book is part of it.

We all have our assignments. Some parts of our assignments are the same. We all need to "love the Lord your God with all your heart and with all your soul and with all your mind... Love your neighbor as yourself." (Matthew 22:37 & 39) We all need to become more like Jesus Christ. We all need to "grow" the fruit of the Spirit (Galatians 5:22-23). We need to put on the armor of God (Ephesians 6:11-13). That's not everything we need to do, but it's enough to let you know what I'm talking about.

At the same time, however, our assignments are different. For example, I have friends who are or have been missionaries in other countries. I also have friends who are highly successful business people. I have friends who are pastors. Some of my friends punch a time clock and raise a family. I have other friends who are professional musicians. Again, you get the idea. All of them are doing their best to fulfill the assignments God gave them.

And me? I am trying to improve my meager musical skills, to write as often as I can, to be an active member of the church I attend, to keep my promises, to honor my commitments, to be a good husband to my wife, to be a good son to my aging father, and maybe another thing or two. If that list gets too big, I won't do justice to any of them and I know God wouldn't like that.

In short, I'm trying to live out a truth I started to learn when I was young. Maybe you have heard it, too. It goes like this - "This little light of mine, I'm going to let it shine. Let it shine, let it shine, let it shine."

In the Sermon on the Mount, Jesus said, "You are the light of the world. A town built on a hill cannot be hidden. Neither do people light a lamp and put it under a bowl. Instead they put it on its stand, and it gives light to everyone in the house. In the same way, let your light shine before others, that they may see your good deeds and glorify your Father in heaven." (Matthew 5:14-16)

So don't let your light go dim; be encouraged and let it shine!

ABOUT THE AUTHOR

CARL BORG is a tax payer, homeowner, comic book enthusiast, church member, musician, writer, husband, son, the founder and President of Wonder Ministries and, most importantly, God's friend.

His desire and ability to communicate in understandable terms helped him become a technical writer, although he spent most of his career in the printed circuit board industry. His love of story, however, had him dreaming of writing novels ever since he was a boy near Lake Minnetonka in Minnesota. He and his wife still live in the area.

AND THE PUBLISHER

Wonder Ministries promotes Christian comic books in several ways. We bring Christian comic books and, whenever possible, a chapel service and a panel discussion about spiritual themes in comics to secular comic book conventions in and near Minneapolis, MN. We also provide expert guidance to church leaders and parents about comic books, both Christian and secular, drawn from over 50 years of exposure and experience in the field. See www.Wonder-Ministries.com for more information.

We also publish Carl's writings. This is his first book, and he's already working on his next one. So is it fiction or not? That would be telling, and we know how to keep a secret.

www.ingramcontent.com/pod-product-compliance
Lightning Source LLC
Chambersburg PA
CBHW070726130626
46553CB00005B/2172